Writing History Essays

For a complete listing of all our titles in this area please visit
www.palgravehighered.com/study-skills

Palgrave Study Skills

Business Degree Success
Career Skills
Cite Them Right (10th edn)
Critical Thinking Skills (2nd edn)
Dissertations and Project Reports
e-Learning Skills (2nd edn)
The Exam Skills Handbook (2nd edn)
Get Sorted
The Graduate Career Guidebook
Great Ways to Learn Anatomy and Physiology
 (2nd edn)
How to Begin Studying English Literature (4th edn)
How to Study Foreign Languages
How to Study Linguistics (2nd edn)
How to Use Your Reading in Your Essays (2nd edn)
How to Write Better Essays (3rd edn)
How to Write Your Undergraduate Dissertation
 (2nd edn)
Improve Your Grammar (2nd edn)
Information Skills
The International Student Handbook
The Mature Student's Guide to Writing (3rd edn)
The Mature Student's Handbook
The Palgrave Student Planner
The Personal Tutor's Handbook
Practical Criticism
Presentation Skills for Students (3rd edn)
The Principles of Writing in Psychology
Professional Writing (3rd edn)
Researching Online
Skills for Success (3rd edn)
Smart Thinking
The Student's Guide to Writing (3rd edn)
The Student Phrase Book
Study Skills Connected
Study Skills for International Postgraduates
Study Skills for Speakers of English as a Second
 Language
The Study Skills Handbook (4th edn)
Studying History (3rd edn)
Studying Law (4th edn)
Studying Modern Drama (2nd edn)
Studying Psychology (2nd edn)

Success in Academic Writing
Teaching Study Skills and Supporting Learning
The Undergraduate Research Handbook
The Work-Based Learning Student Handbook
 (2nd edn)
Work Placements – A Survival Guide for Students
Write it Right (2nd edn)
Writing for Engineers (3rd edn)
Writing for Law
Writing for Nursing and Midwifery Students
 (2nd edn)
Writing History Essays (2nd edn)
You2Uni: Decide. Prepare. Apply

Pocket Study Skills

14 Days to Exam Success
Analyzing a Case Study
Brilliant Writing Tips for Students
Completing Your PhD
Doing Research
Getting Critical (2nd edn)
Planning Your Dissertation
Planning Your Essay (2nd edn)
Planning Your PhD
Posters and Presentations
Reading and Making Notes (2nd edn)
Referencing and Understanding Plagiarism
Reflective Writing
Report Writing
Science Study Skills
Studying with Dyslexia
Success in Groupwork
Time Management
Where's Your Argument?
Writing for University (2nd edn)

Palgrave Career Skills

Excel at Graduate Interviews
Graduate Entrepreneurship
How to Succeed at Assessment Centres
Social Media for your Student and Graduate
 Job Search
Work Experience, Placements and Internships

Writing
History
Essays

2nd edition

Ian Mabbett

 palgrave

First edition 2006
Second edition 2016
Published by
PALGRAVE

Palgrave in the UK is an imprint of Macmillan Publishers Limited, registered in England, company number 785998, of 4 Crinan Street, London, N1 9XW.

Palgrave Macmillan in the US is a division of St Martin's Press LLC, 175 Fifth Avenue, New York, NY 10010.

Palgrave is a global imprint of the above companies and is represented throughout the world.

Palgrave® and Macmillan® are registered trademarks in the United States, the United Kingdom, Europe and other countries.

ISBN 978–1–137–54366–0 paperback

This book is printed on paper suitable for recycling and made from fully managed and sustained forest sources. Logging, pulping and manufacturing processes are expected to conform to the environmental regulations of the country of origin.

A catalogue record for this book is available from the British Library.

A catalog record for this book is available from the Library of Congress.

Printed and bound by CPI Group (UK) Ltd, Croydon, CR0 4YY

Contents

Author's Note

In this book several choices needed to be made in matters of word usage, especially where conventions differ among English-speaking countries. Generally, I have sought words not likely to be obscure to those familiar with either British or American vocabulary. Thus 'teacher' is preferred to both 'tutor' and 'professor'. I have, however, consistently used the term 'essay' to designate the sort of writing that requires historical argument and independent thought. Many readers will be better acquainted with other expressions such as 'term paper' or 'research paper', but a major concern of the book is with the writing of assignments, short or long, which have the character of apprenticeship exercises in historical practice, and 'essay' appears to be the best generic term for this. Chapter 2 should make this concern clear.

In Chapter 12 on documentation conventions, comments and examples are offered concerning citation systems likely to be familiar to readers on both sides of the Atlantic.

I would like to thank very cordially those who gave me the benefit of their advice or assistance while this book was in preparation; naturally nobody other than I bears responsibility for errors or defects. Special thanks are due to Gordon Taylor, who took considerable trouble to go through the entire manuscript in detail and made numerous helpful suggestions. I am most grateful also for the valuable comments and suggestions made by Mike Godley, Kate Brittlebank, the anonymous referees reporting for the publishers, and Mark Peel, whose work on the departmental guidelines for history students in Monash University inspired some of the material used here. I have benefited especially from having had the leisure to complete the first edition of this book during part of my tenure of membership at the Institute for Advanced Study, Princeton, in 2005–06. During this period I was supported by funds from the Friends of the Institute for Advanced Study. Finally, I would like to acknowledge the helpfulness and professionalism of the publishers at all stages in the preparation of this book for publication.

Preface to the Second Edition

In the preparation of the second edition, I have benefited from the suggestions of various readers who have used this book, and hope that the changes now made will be helpful. These include some simplification and abridgement in places, and the addition of some material, notably in the chapters on the use of online sources and the writing of theses, and in the appendix on historiography.

In this work of revision, I have been helped especially by the wise counsel and practical advice of Professor David Garrioch, of Monash University, who offered valuable suggestions for use in the new sections written for this edition. I would like to reiterate my grateful appreciation of the encouragement and support given by the publishers.

I.W. Mabbett
January 2016

Chapter 1

A History Essay is History

Chapter overview

► The historian seeks facts, but they are elusive and obscure at first.
► History is all about 'debate and conflicting evidence'.
► History is a craft – it is about doing, not just seeing.
► History is an art – it requires imagination and creativity.
► History seeks understanding by exploring the *context* in time and space, and context expands indefinitely.
► A definition of history: the study of the past through the critical appraisal of recorded words.
► History differs in method and content from its various neighbouring disciplines.
► Social sciences seek increasingly exact measurements; history cannot avoid fuzziness in places.

Now, what I want is, Facts. Teach these boys and girls nothing but Facts. Facts alone are wanted in life.[1]

I took the book list and the essay title, found the Radcliffe Camera [a library building at the University of Oxford at the time], began to read and perceived that I had been entirely misled for six years: history is fact only up to a point – more crucially, it is a matter of debate and conflicting evidence. It was like some kind of divine revelation: I went into the Camera a heathen and came out converted, but thought little of it, settling effortlessly into a new understanding, which is something that you can do at 18.[2]

History is, frankly, the most humane of subjects. The discipline of trying to understand the past and the character of change isn't narrowly vocational – it provides an intensive training in critical thinking and communication, a portfolio of skills and sensitivities that can be applied to any walk of life.[3]

The first quotation above contains the famous words introducing Dickens' novel *Hard Times*, spoken by a man who thinks only facts matter. This belief is rejected by the novelist Penelope Lively in the second quotation; for her, history is fact only up to a point. Real history is 'debate and conflicting evidence'. This does not mean that facts are unimportant. Historians love facts; they go through every manner of hardship tracing facts across all terrains and in all weathers. The mistake they do not make is to suppose that facts are easily found, and, when found, perceived to be clear and certain, as if made of stone. On the contrary, historical facts are remarkably elusive and commonly retreat into the undergrowth, leaving only ambiguous traces that require skill to interpret. They are real, but the evidence by which they may come to be known can never be exhaustively ascertained; we can never completely know them. It is working on history essays that brings the student most directly into a vivid and dynamic confrontation with 'debate and conflicting evidence'. This is why writing essays is so important; it fosters 'the training in critical thinking and communication' emphasized by Rees Davies in the third quotation above.

The practice of history is a craft

The study of history does not consist simply of learning facts. It involves a close encounter with debate and conflicting evidence. It involves manipulating ideas and interpretations, testing hypotheses, acquiring skill. You learn with your muscles, not just your eyes – that is, by doing, not just by seeing. You find out what history is by putting it into practice.

So the chief focus will be on active processes in which techniques are developed – reading for an essay, planning, drafting, revising, and then learning to do even better next time. It is a series of activities that teach by experience; it is a craft.

There is no substitute for experience, and the real learning process must take place in specific courses of study. This book offers advice about the techniques of historical craft; the practical application and the consequent learning are up to you.

History is also an art

These remarks may suggest that historical study follows a set of rules; but this needs to be qualified. No set of rules can by itself guarantee success in historical study and writing. The advice given here must always be adapted to practical experience. Anything in the following pages may be modified or even discarded by a teacher in accordance with the practical needs of a particular course of study. Nothing that follows here is to be treated as a rule that will make it impossible to go wrong.

Essays are judged essentially by how well their writers have understood what they have read and how well they can respond critically, economically and elegantly to that understanding. The literal-minded observance of rules can be an obstacle to these qualities. An essay is not a set of rote procedures like the routine checks made by a pilot before taking his[4] craft into the air. An essay is unique; it should show originality and independence. It requires your own critical thought, responding to the nuances of the sources you have read, seeing implicit connections between facts and ideas, clarifying the essentials of a problem, even finding a new and interesting way of looking at it.

So you should cultivate originality and independent thought. But how? What about the details, the nuts-and-bolts problems of writing essays? How do you decide where to start? How much factual information is required? When is a footnote needed? How do you know when you have written enough? Such questions need answers. There is a need for guidelines to steer you through the problems of historical study.

This book will offer such guidelines, but guidelines are not iron rules. In later years, you may have forgotten all the details, but still be able to write good history essays. What makes essays good is not the rules they mechanically follow. Guidelines can support your work, like crutches, while the muscles of insight and judgment grow strong. Eventually, the crutches can be thrown away and you can step out independently; the rules you have learned will have blended into an instinct for what is obviously right.

A history essay is history

Why need there be a manual for study and writing in history, as distinct from English literature or philosophy or any other branch of the humanities?[5] After all, good methods that work for one subject ought to work for another. This is true. What makes any essay good is the quality of the thought behind it, rather than its success in applying particular rules of history or any other discipline. However, different sorts of thought are needed for different disciplines.

So what is special and particular about history? This ought to be an easy question, but in fact historians all answer it in different ways.

Historians, like any other human group, develop their own working culture with its unquestioned assumptions and its prejudices. Newcomers need to find out what these assumptions are, but may find it surprisingly difficult to get satisfactory answers to their questions ('How do I avoid plagiarism?' 'Do I have to give evidence for this statement?'). Historians, anxious to share with students their own intellectual delight in the most advanced and sophisticated approaches in historical research, may take the basics too much for granted. Explaining rudiments that one learned many years ago may prove difficult. The famous verse about the centipede encapsulates this difficulty:

> A centipede was happy quite,
> Until a toad in fun
> Said 'Pray which leg moves after which?'
> And worked her mind to such a pitch,
> She lay distracted in the ditch
> Considering how to run.[6]

Defining history

So, when historians try to explain what history is, they say many different things. Often they automatically offer advanced theoretical speculation rather than practical advice about the rudiments. Much has been written about the meaning of history, including debates about whether history can hope to find 'truth', and other more or less philosophical issues. These discussions, although important, are not the same thing as the basic rudiments of the subject, which are what concern us here.

What, then, is it that history basically does? An example will help. Below are four paragraphs on Machiavelli's political philosophy, which recommends to a ruler a tough, cynical approach to government. A historian could possibly have written any of these passages, but just one of them is basically historical. Which one? None is supposed to be better than the others – they are designed to illustrate different approaches, not superior technique. Which is the most *historical* one, and what makes it historical? It is worth taking time to look at the paragraphs and think about them, because the differences between them help to show how history is different from other disciplines.

1 Machiavelli accepted the principle that a state's survival transcends the interests of the individuals within it; this justifies all measures necessary to secure the state's survival. Upon this principle he erected a consistent and realistic, if harsh, theory of government that offered guidelines for a ruler. Like *The Prince* or not, we have to accept that Machiavelli's political philosophy is grounded in scientific observation.

2 We do not know enough about Machiavelli's childhood to understand properly how it may have affected his later outlook and values. However, we do know something about him that could have had a big effect on him – the effect of being held prisoner and tortured. Studies of

the psychology of stress show how trauma can shape deep-seated attitudes and determine an individual's whole construction of reality. Machiavelli's views of politics were inevitably influenced by his experience of imprisonment by the Medici.

3 Machiavelli's policies can be judged by the standards of several theories. According to a consequentialist theory, the value of an action is determined by the total of its results; if a ruler's policies result in the killing of innocent people but rapidly end a war, the harm done may be less than if no such policy had been followed, and justify Machiavelli's policy. A theory of categorical imperatives, on the other hand, may forbid killing innocent people regardless of the later consequences, and Machiavelli stands condemned. Again, Buddhist ethics might judge a deed by what is in the mind of its perpetrator: if a ruler's intentions were genuinely benevolent, this might excuse actions with harmful consequences.

4 Perhaps, if France and Spain had been superpowers threatening each other with nuclear weapons, conflict in Italy would have been kept in check by powerful kingdoms restraining their small client states from fear of mutual assured destruction, and Machiavelli would have lived in a more peaceful world with different rules of political behaviour. As it was, there was no such constraint. Northern Italian states were freely preyed on by the armies of bigger kingdoms and constantly disrupted by outside interference. No local state could hope for a stable and peaceful system of international relations. This is the environment which[7] shaped Machiavelli's perceptions.

The four different comments here represent four different approaches to the study of Machiavelli, showing the methods and assumptions of four different academic disciplines. Just one of them places itself squarely within the domain of historical study.

Paragraph 1 treats him as a contributor to the philosophy or science of politics, discussing his views within a range of theoretical ideas about international politics. Whether or not it is a good contribution, the paragraph looks like political science.

Paragraph 2, by contrast, focuses narrowly on what went on inside Machiavelli. A historian might do this, but the paragraph appeals to psychological studies which relate severe stress to behaviour; it is thus basically psychology.

Paragraph 3 is, on the other hand, not about the way in which Machiavelli came to have his ideas (either by perceiving correctly the way things worked, or by having had certain experiences); it takes the ideas as given and considers whether they are good or bad. It thus identifies itself as moral philosophy.

We are left with paragraph 4, which accounts for Machiavelli's ideas by relating them to his historical environment. This shows the most clearly historical approach because it seeks to explain particular things (in this case, Machiavelli's ideas) within their own environment: where he lived, peace and stability were unobtainable, and this placed limits on what could be considered politically possible. Historians start with the particular environment of the object of study. They focus on the ways in which something is influenced by events in its own context. This is in contrast to paragraph 1, which talks about universal factors, not the particular context of northern Italy.

Thus, historical study begins with questions about the particular – a book, an idea, a person, a series of events, anything identifiable through historical sources. We examine it in its context, in its own environment; the context examined may broaden to include anything at all that might be relevant. We may look at earlier or later times to see whether similar causes produced similar results in other cases. However, when the broadening of context leads us into theories, for example about politics in general or the workings of the mind in general, we are moving into another discipline, such as political science or psychology. The main thing to remember is that history starts from the close examination of particular objects of study, seeking understanding of them within their own contexts.

This lays the groundwork for the task of defining history. Let us identify three stages:

Definition 1 History is the past.

This is true, but not helpful. The word 'history' refers sometimes to the past, sometimes to the study of it. What we are looking for in order to compare history with anthropology, music, linguistics and so on is a definition of a type of study:

Definition 2 History is the study of the past.

The problem with this is that any event whatsoever becomes past as soon as it has happened. Literature is past words. Observations of stars are observations of past events (often long past). Anthropologists may use the 'ethnographic present' tense in their writing, but for all that they are describing systems of thought and behaviour which were observed in the past, and may well be changing now (perhaps even as a result of the disruption caused by the anthropologist's presence). Geologists may find out about the history of the earth's crust from examination of ancient rock layers in the present.

What we need is something like this:

Definition 3 History is the study of the past through the critical appraisal of recorded words.

There is indeed an objection to this definition. Historians often study the past through the appraisal of things other than words, and such research includes some of the most interesting developments today.

Historians have been turning from their archives to the scrutiny of art and architecture, costumes and customs, rituals and recreations, diet and demography, indeed to any sort of interaction between people and their physical environment, often with the most rewarding results.[8] A historian of social history through cinema may turn from the recorded words of the talkies to the images of the silent film, without ceasing to be a historian.

However, the apprentice in any art or craft must start by learning about the techniques and principles at the core of the subject; it is these which have given shape and structure to the practice of the vocation. The beginner must start with the basic techniques and principles.

The masters in the trade may have developed advanced techniques which do not obey the rules of the core principles. Meanwhile, however, the beginner is likely to end in confusion if he tries to jump to the most new and advanced sorts of practice. It is the old fallacy of seeking to run before you can walk. Therefore, it is best to leave the exceptions on one side and attend first to the core structures and principles.

History and its neighbouring disciplines

History is distinguished as a discipline, then, by the fact that its evidence typically consists of recorded words. The evidence may be in any form: books, newspapers, diaries, archives, bills, bus tickets, film soundtracks, tape-recorded interviews, shorthand notes, inscriptions on stone or tortoise-shell, or any other form of recorded words. For the historian, the record is a *source* or document, and *documentation* is the identification of these sources as verifiable evidence.

What the historian appraises critically is what his sources say. That is, he is interested in the meaning of the words, rather than in, say, their handwriting, or the chemical composition of the fabric on which they are recorded. History is about the meaning of what is written in the sources, and the light they throw on what was going on when they were written. Historical understanding advances by moving back and forth between the written sources and knowledge about the environments in which they were produced; each can help with the understanding of the other.

Various other disciplines stand close beside history, and the experienced historian may sometimes or often wish to raid them for what they may yield. The student does not need to worry about these other disciplines, at least in the earlier stages. However, some of them need at least to be recognized:

- When the words of the document are in a language not the historian's own, he must double as a *linguist*. Most of the history of the world is of places that did not use English.

- *Philology* may be needed to interpret sources in dead or literary languages. This is the study of languages with attention to their historical development and the relations between them. In practice, philologists tend to be especially proficient in ancient languages, and it is a knowledge of these that is required for the history of the remoter past (e.g. Old English for early English history, Latin for European, Sanskrit for Indian).

- The historian may use as evidence any written sources, including literature generally; thus historical sources overlap those of *literary criticism*, but for the historian they are used in a different way.

- *Archaeology* is the study of the past using any sort of physical object as evidence, not just objects under the ground. Industrial archaeology, for example, studies buildings, sites, artefacts and any other physical evidence shedding light on the making, transport and use of products of any sort.

- *Epigraphy* is the study of inscriptions, typically on stone or metal. These are important for the study of periods when writing was known, but all writings on perishable materials such as paper have vanished.

- *Palaeography* is the study of the formation of characters and styles of writing at different periods in the past, by which, for example, a document may be roughly dated even if the date is not otherwise known.

- *Diplomatics* is the scientific study of written documents addressed to their physical characteristics; it includes forensic analysis of ink and paper which can yield facts of historical interest about date, authenticity and provenance. For example, a massive hoax during the 1980s involved the production of a large set of 'diaries' purporting to be Hitler's. The hoax, at first successful, was uncovered only after proper forensic examination became possible; for example, the ink used was of a type not available to Hitler, and measurement of the evaporation of chloride in the ink showed that the writings were too recent to be authentic. Here, diplomatic analysis aided history.

- *Social sciences,* such as *sociology, political science, psychology* and *economics*, often overlap in sources or subject matter with history, but their methods are different. There are sometimes subtle points of similarity and difference between mainstream history and historical topics in various other disciplines such as economics or anthropology. More comments on history and social sciences appear below.

Scholars in different disciplines often use each other's techniques; this lies behind many interesting developments in research, but it can be risky, and should not to be attempted lightly by the student.

Social sciences, humanities and fuzziness

Disciplines that are concerned with the study of people, culture and society can be divided into two classes: social sciences and humanities. (As noted above, the 'humanities' roughly correspond to liberal arts.) Sometimes history is regarded as a social science, sometimes not. How we regard it is quite important for our understanding of how it works.

Social sciences, unlike physical sciences, concern human society, but they are (partly) distinguished from the humanities because they seek to use scientific methods. They ask questions which can be answered fairly precisely by measurement. Thus, the degree of poverty or disease in a particular place or time is something which can be measured, so long as good enough statistics are available. Poverty and disease can then be compared in different places and times. Such measurements and comparisons belong to the studies of economics and sociology, which are core social science disciplines.

The humanities, by contrast, are concerned with culture, especially language and literature. Written documents and art forms are typical sources. Understanding is sought through refining ideas about the meaning of what is studied rather than through measurement of it. Ideas are not like statistics; they have fuzzy boundaries.

History can concern itself with questions belonging to both social sciences and the humanities. It cannot be decisively classified as of one type and not the other. However, it has deep roots in the humanities, and its core categories have fuzzy boundaries.

'Were more people literate in the eighteenth than in the seventeenth century?' is a question that can be answered by statistics, if they are available. But what happens if they are not? Then it is necessary to seek more indirect evidence, using inspired detective work; and this requires an imaginative search for clues among all sorts of historical sources.

'Was the frequency of wars in northern Italy a major influence on Machiavelli's thought?' cannot really be answered by statistics. The answer will not depend mechanically on a precise total of numbers of wars. It will depend in all sorts of ways on the character, frequency and effects of wars. There is no obvious way of measuring all the different ways in which warfare could affect people's minds and influence their worldview, or of deciding what would count as 'major'. In a sense, then, the idea of the frequency of wars as an influence on Machiavelli has fuzzy boundaries.

The importance of fuzziness cannot be overemphasized. It does not mean lack of rigour. The reason why a historian cannot put a percentage value on the importance of the frequency of wars in northern Italy to Machiavelli's thought is not that his method is sloppy; it lies in the nature of the question. Human ideas and behaviour might be influenced by anything at all within people's experience. The historian can seldom be sure that *all* the evidence that might be relevant has, in fact, been collected. The rigour lies in the thoroughness of the detective work conducted, not in the precision of calculations made using known facts.

History will always use statistics and precise measurements where these are relevant and available, but it will also want to explore the background, asking difficult questions about the effects of these measured quantities upon culture and experience. History will also be keenly interested in questioning how trustworthy the statistics are, looking into the ways in which they were collected and the behaviour of the people who produced and used them. A historical task is rarely completed when a column of figures has been added; real understanding usually requires more attention to human experience and behaviour.

So historical argument in a piece of research, or a student essay, does not take the form of formal proof, in the manner of an algebraic equation. On the contrary, it may always be challenged on the basis of further evidence. Evidence is all-important; the more of it there is, the better; but we should never think that we know it *all*.

One last point that will be worth recalling later: the writing of a historical argument (for example, in an essay) is *a dialogue with the sources*. It discusses the detective work that has gone into assessing them in order to provide material for the argument. Therefore, it must explain its conclusions about the value of the sources as well as its conclusions about the problem being discussed. These two sorts of explanation cannot always conveniently be carried on at once, and for clarity it is often necessary to separate the explanations of the value of sources in footnotes. This point is taken up in Chapter 12 (see p. 127).

The wavelength of history

This book is all about history as something with its own special character, different from sociology or economics or literature or any other discipline. How is it different? It is important to develop some idea about what makes history special. What this chapter may help you realize is how very *concrete* history is. It is all about the actual evidence from which you can learn about people's actual ideas and behaviour. However far the historian may move away from the concrete sources into abstract generalizations or theories (and many historians are fascinated by big theories), the documentary evidence is always exerting a pull on his mind, and, in the end, what justifies his conclusions is his ability to show convincingly the value of the sources on which they depend.

Almost any statement about the past can be used in illustration. Here is one (that is discussed further in chapter 15):

> The Indian emperor Akbar set out to disprove the doctrine of the court religious teachers that human beings are given speech by a divine gift, not by learning.

For most disciplines, this sentence would be taken as solid evidence, capable of being used as a building block in an argument. The student of religions would be interested in the theory of divine intervention in human affairs, the student of politics in the relationship between royal power and the authority of religious teachers and so on. But the historian automatically and instinctively turns, not to the theories – they come much later in his programme – but to the *evidence for the statement*.

He asks: 'How do we know this?', and immediately, rolling up his shirtsleeves, so to speak, burrows into the documentary evidence. Instead of taking the statement and using it as a building block for theory, he pulls it to pieces. 'What documentary source tells us this about Akbar? Who wrote it? Why? For whom? What does it tell us about the author? Did he have any axe to grind?' These are the historical questions which set the historian off on a quest that leads in the opposite direction to that taken by most other specialists.

If it turns out that the document making this claim about Akbar is misleading or untrustworthy, the comparative religionists, political scientists and the rest might lose interest, but that is just where the historian feels that things are becoming interesting. '*Why* is the document misleading? What do we learn about society and politics in the India of the time from the fact that the author is not to be trusted? If he was biased, what gave him that bias? What was it *like* to be in the imperial court at that time?'

Thus, when you write history essays, you may make many generalizations and develop interest in theories, but they must always be anchored to an analysis of the actual hard evidence that is as detailed and specific as your time and your sources will allow. That is what makes your work history.

Questions

1 At the start of the chapter is quoted the view that history is a 'training in critical thinking and communication, a portfolio of skills and sensitivities that can be applied to any walk of life'. Is this borne out at all by your own experience? Does this view seem plausible to you, or might it be exaggerated?

2 Sometimes in schools history is taught in combination with other subjects such as geography or cultural studies. Is there anything wrong with this? How good an argument can be made for the case that history is unique and should be studied as a separate subject?

3 Should history be thought of as a sort of science?

A History Essay is More than Just History

Chapter overview

► Four basic facts about history essays: they are history, academic writing, essays, literature.

► Academic writing uses the best sources available, provides verifiable documentation, and seeks to require the reader to reach the same conclusions as the writer by proper reasoning from public evidence.

► The principle of best available sources is that history writing must use the best sources available to the writer within the conditions that limit the task.

► An essay is a statement of what the writer thinks.

► Independent thought is absolutely essential to an essay; otherwise it is not a statement of what the writer thinks.

► Literature demands both style and accuracy. Good history writing in English cannot exist without good English writing.

The real nature of history essays can be summed up by just four fundamental principles. Chapter 1 was concerned with the first of these: a history essay is *history*. This seems obvious, but, as the chapter showed, there are subtleties. This chapter will introduce the other three. It is a bird's-eye view of the terrain to be explored further in later chapters. The four fundamental principles of the history essay are as follows:

1 It is **history**.
2 It is **academic**.
3 It is **an essay**.
4 It is **literature**.

A history essay is academic writing

What makes writing academic?

How is academic writing different from other sorts? Here are some of the ways in which students have tried to explain it. Most of them are, in fact, misleading; you can consider them and decide which, if any, catch the essential difference:

1　Academic writing cannot be simple, readable and attractive in style, because its subject matter makes it difficult to read.
2　It is based on research; non-academic writing is not.
3　It argues for a point of view; non-academic writing basically just describes things.
4　Non-academic writing often asserts a point of view, but academic writing must strike a balance between different points of view.
5　It deals with subjects of serious importance to our understanding of the world.
6　What makes it academic is its logical manner of argument, not the importance of the subject matter.
7　It must offer evidence for all the claims it makes; non-academic writing need not.
8　Academic writing must supply detailed argument, not broad generalizations.
9　It must focus on one particular question, whereas non-academic writing can bring together any number of questions.
10　It has footnotes.

Which of these answers is best?

Most of the discussion of these answers will be left for you. However, the first one calls for an immediate comment. Unfortunately, academic writing is too often difficult to read. There is no good reason why it should be. Perhaps this should be qualified: some disciplines, not usually history, need to create their own technical terms – jargon – in order to analyse their subject matter precisely. The more jargon there is, the more difficult it generally is to read. Many disciplines (including history), however, can usually stick to straightforward language, and any reasonably educated person should have no difficulty following it. The first listed answer above, therefore, is wrong.

As for the others, most identify some genuine characteristics of academic writing. However, most of them fail to identify just what it is that distinguishes the academic from the non-academic: nearly all of them attribute to academic writing characteristics also found plentifully in journalism or other forms of writing which make no claim to academic scholarship whatsoever.

What, then, really makes the difference? The difference, which should be carefully noticed, is this. In a non-academic essay you write what you think about the topic. In an academic essay, you write what you think and also seek to *compel the reader to think the same, arguing by proper reasoning from public evidence.*

This leads to recognition of two linked principles of academic writing: verifiability and documentation.

1 *Verifiability*: Public evidence is evidence that the reader could verify for himself. It has been created in a laboratory, or seen through a telescope or microscope, or dug up, or observed somewhere. Thus, the reader of what you write should be able to verify your evidence by going to the place where the evidence is – library, museum, archives and so on. If the evidence is sound, he must then find himself compelled by it and your argument to agree with your conclusions.

2 *Documentation*: All the evidence that actually played a part in leading you to your conclusion *must* be identified and made verifiable to your reader in order that, if he wishes, it may do the same for him. So the verifiability principle means that it is not enough to say simply that there is evidence for whatever you claim as fact. If you wish to compel your reader to draw the same conclusions as you have drawn, you must make it possible for the reader to inspect the evidence for your conclusions, and you must *cite your evidence adequately and accurately.*

Thus, points 7 and 10 in the list above, given a suitable explanation on the lines just discussed, together come closest to the correct answer. Every discipline has its own conventions for the documentation of evidence, normally in a footnote that contains the details necessary for verification. Some good journalism is based on solid research and beats the academics at their own game, but the essential difference is that, as journalism, it is not required to provide verifiable documentation for all its claims.

To be sure, not *all* types of academic writing are marked by rigorous documentation. Exceptions include textbooks, reflective essays, review articles, lectures, formal conference addresses and so on. (We could call them 'non-core' academic activities.) But these other things could not be written to a proper standard without building on the core tradition of rigorously documented research publications, which displays the essentials of the craft.

An essay is judged in relation to its sources

Verifiability is not the same thing as *proving your conclusions to be true*. Essays cannot normally be expected to prove the truth of their statements. But they can be expected to *demonstrate that particular statements based on particular sources are justified*. Thus, whatever you say is to be judged wholly in relation to the best sources you can use. So long as you make an effort to examine the best sources available, your essay will be judged according to its success in demonstrating the reasonableness of conclusions based *just on these sources,* not the conclusions that might be based on all the sources which exist anywhere.

The principle of best available sources

What is the difference between academic research and the writing of a student essay? Academic research attempts ideally to consult *all* the important relevant sources; preparation of a student essay is limited to an arbitrarily limited range of sources that are readily available. It is an apprenticeship exercise. Within this range, use *the best ones.*

What makes a good essay good is not just a particular argument or a particular set of facts, such as could easily be found in an encyclopedia, for example. A good essay must show discrimination in seeking out evidence from the sources most likely to yield a rich harvest of evidence which contributes to an understanding of the topic. A school encyclopedia, for example, will carry little weight. A quotation from an internet source will carry none unless you can explain what gives it authority. Use primary sources when you can. Seek books or articles based on original research, with proper documentation.

Remember that historical research involves exploring the context of a topic in quest of evidence, and contexts have fuzzy edges – they expand to fill the whole of human experience. Your job is to minimize the chance that your argument could be upset by another piece of evidence from some other source. A brief encyclopedia article may not alert you to important pieces of evidence demanding attention; a recently published book packed with research results is more likely to mention things mattering to your argument, for or against. That is why you need to use the best possible array of sources.

A history essay is an essay

So essays are history, and they are academic. But what is an essay? This is more important, and less obvious, than is often thought. The points in this section matter.

An essay, whether literary or academic, is not the same thing as a collection of information, such as might be assigned in a school exercise. Let us call such an exercise a 'report'. Some documents called 'reports' are written by experts who are paid well to study serious problems and propose solutions, but, for our immediate purpose, what is meant by a report is a routine information-gathering or scrapbook exercise which might be conducted at a computer with internet access or in a local library. In such a report you collect certain facts or ideas for a particular purpose; your own ideas do not necessarily have to play a part in what you write.

An essay is quite different. It is *a statement of what you think*. It is not a statement of what other people think, although you may refer to what other people think as evidence or as authority to support your reasoning. You are entitled to express any thoughts whatsoever. It does not matter what they are. What matters is that the essay expresses what *you* think about something.

In this book, the term 'essay' is used in this general sense, to identify a type of literature as just defined. The term is also used to designate a type of student assignment in some universities but not others; other designations identify particular different types of essay, such as 'term paper', 'research paper' and so on. The term 'essay', as used here, applies to any sort of student assignment which can be called an essay in the general sense, requiring the writer to express independent thought.

Independent thought

Here is a simple exercise intended to emphasize the importance of independent thought. Which of the three passages below best illustrates the qualities expected in good essay writing?

Imagine that the essay is set to answer the question: 'How far was the American Revolution a social revolution?' The imaginary student writing the essay has read the following passage from a book:

> Although no social revolution occurred in America in the 1770s, the American Revolution could not have unfolded when or as it did without the self-conscious action of urban laboring people from the bottom and middle strata who became convinced that they must either create power where none had existed before or watch their position deteriorate, in both absolute and relative terms.

Here are three passages from imaginary answers:

> A. Although no social revolution occurred in America in the 1770s, the American Revolution could not have unfolded when or as it did without the self-conscious action of urban laboring people from the bottom and middle strata who became convinced that they must either create power where none had existed before or watch their position deteriorate, in both absolute and relative terms.[1]

> 1. Gary B. Nash, *The Urban Crucible: The Northern Seaports and the Origins of the American Revolution*, abridged edn, Cambridge, MA: Harvard University Press, 1986, p. 247

B. Although, in the 1770s, there was no social revolution in America, the American Revolution could not have developed in the way it did without the self-aware action of urban working people from the bottom and middle layers who became convinced that they must either make power or look at their position deteriorate, both absolutely and relatively.[1]

1. Gary B. Nash, *The Urban Crucible: The Northern Seaports and the Origins of the American Revolution*, abridged edn, Cambridge, MA: Harvard University Press, 1986, p. 247

C. The 1770s may not have been marked by a thoroughgoing social revolution, but Nash has argued that there were massive changes going on all the same; many working people in the cities he studied, in his view, saw themselves as becoming poorer or failing to benefit from opportunities seized by the wealthy, and they judged that the only solution lay in making a bid to change the structure of power.[1]

1. Gary B. Nash, *The Urban Crucible: The Northern Seaports and the Origins of the American Revolution*, abridged edn, Cambridge, MA: Harvard University Press, 1986, p. 247

We may notice first one good point common to all: they all properly cite the source depended on by supplying the correct details in a footnote. But, beyond this, we are concerned with the quality of the thought going into what the essay has to say.

The first passage does not tell you what the student thinks. The words offered are not the expression of the writer's thoughts; they are just copied from a book. No thought is involved. But an essay must express the writer's own thought; so this passage cannot count as real essay writing. The essay in which it appears is likely to be rejected altogether on account of plagiarism.

The second changes some of the words used by the source. A passage copied from what was written by somebody else, with some of the words changed, does not go very far towards telling you what the writer thinks. It does not count as an essay. If you take a cake made by somebody else, cut some bits out of it, and stick some fragments from other people's cakes into the gaps, you have not made a cake. Similarly, this passage is worthless.

The third contains different words, and is arranged to express the student's own understanding of what is claimed in the book used. The student is using his own words to describe the ideas which come from reading the passage, thereby expressing his own understanding of it, even if he does not add much that is new. (For a longer example showing how value is added by the deployment of the student's independent thought, see the end of Chapter 10.) The mere fact that this passage expresses the writer's own understanding of what the author says qualifies it as part of an essay, so it must be worth a lot more than either of the other passages, which do not even begin to offer anything by way of independent thought that can be judged.

So, when you are asked to write a history essay about a given question, you are expected to write down some ideas that come to *your* mind when you read the sources. True, some of the essay may consist of factual description of the evidence, much as may occur in a report, but this description belongs in your essay only to the extent that it *serves the purpose of justifying and supporting your own thought*. The principle of independent thought in essay writing will be taken up in Chapter 10, where these issues are discussed in greater detail (pp. 94–7).

A history essay is literature

The literary quality of an essay matters as much as that of any other piece of writing. Many of the qualities which count most in making your argument easy to follow and the ideas palatable to entertain are literary qualities. The writing must be good enough to carry the reader with you.

Sometimes, students feel insecure about writing an academic essay and suppose that, to be sufficiently academic, what they write must somehow resemble whichever of the books they have read was most difficult to understand. But prose style is not a matter of writing long complicated sentences or displaying an impressive vocabulary; it is a matter of finding the best words for your purposes, and the best style is often, although not always, the simplest – the words are so right that the meaning is completely transparent, and the reader is not conscious of anything that can be called 'style' coming between the author's intention and his own understanding.

Readers wish to be able to hear speaking through the prose an individual voice, one that expresses its author's own thoughts with clarity, economy, fidelity, simplicity and, preferably, also some grace and elegance. So what really counts in good writing, then, is not just its avoidance of inaccuracies in grammar, spelling and so on, but also the literary quality of its style.

However, this is not to say that accuracy in English does not matter. Inaccuracy is commonly the companion of obscure or sloppy thought processes; it quite often leads to ambiguity, and sometimes to obscurity, compelling the reader to reread and reread to work out the meaning; and it tends strongly to distract the reader from the flow of ideas, especially if the reader is required to mark errors on the script. Correct English is one part of good English. The topic is dealt with more fully in Chapter 13.

Questions

1 At the start of this chapter is a list of attempts to define academic writing. Points 7 and 10 are recommended as the most accurate. Among the others, which are the worst and the best?

2 In historical research, what are the limits of attempts to prove claims true?

3 Here is a passage about the Chinese attitude towards the past, from Simon Leys, *The Angel and the Octopus*, Sydney: Duffy and Snellgrove, 1999, pp. 15f.:

> Confucius considered Antiquity as a repository of all human values. Therefore, according to him, the Sage's mission was not to *create* anything anew, but merely to *transmit* the heritage of the Ancients. In actual fact, such a program was far less conservative than might first appear ... the Antiquity to which he referred was a *lost* Antiquity, which the Sage had to seek and practically to *reinvent*. ... What was meant by these semantic conventions practically amounted to the exact opposite: their so-called 'Antiquity' referred to a mythical Golden Age – actually their utopian vision of the *future* – whereas the so-called 'modern practices' referred to the inheritance of the recent past; that is, in fact, the *real past*.

Imagine that you are writing an essay on the Chinese attitude to the past, and compose a sentence in which you use Simon Leys' remarks as a source, with an appropriate footnote.

The History Essay as a Process

Chapter overview

▶ Work on any history essay must begin with a question.

▶ An essay question must be challenging – it concerns something surprising, unexplained and not obvious.

▶ The design of a history essay must incorporate five elements: a question, an introduction, factual evidence, critical assessment of the evidence and sources, and a conclusion.

▶ Read as much as possible, exploiting every opportunity to maximize use of libraries and other routes to historical sources.

▶ While reading, speculate actively about possible pathways to conclusions, asking constantly branching questions.

▶ Historical study must foster independent thought.

History begins with a question …

Any historical enquiry must begin with a carefully expressed question. One dangerous mistake is to suppose that the wording of the essay title is unimportant – that it is just a springboard from which to leap into a particular topic, find out what you can, and report on it. But an essay is not a report. It is a statement of what you think. This thought is good or bad only through *its success in responding to a particular question*. Your essay is no essay at all except insofar as it does this.

Essay titles as questions: many or most essay titles are in the form of questions, or can easily be turned into questions. If you are given a title that does not obviously raise a question, it is important to turn it into one in your mind as you work; *you must never work without actively looking for answers to specific questions*. The question set, if it is to seem right, must be in a special sense *interesting*. That is, the answer to it is not obvious. There is something which, at first sight, seems surprising – it teases the intellect, it demands engagement. The topic set must have some catch in it, something that makes it interesting.

Here are some examples:

- 'Peter the Great's modernization of Russia' becomes 'How [or in what ways] did Peter the Great modernize Russia?' Can it really be true that one man, Peter the Great, effectively modernized a vast country? We need to understand what is meant by 'modernization' and how far it really changed things in Russia.

- 'The granting to women of the right to vote in Switzerland' becomes 'Why did Swiss women not get the right to vote in federal elections until 1971?' It seems surprising that it happened so late. What, then, were the special conditions in Switzerland that might explain the delay?

- 'The real standard of living of industrial workers in England in the first half of the nineteenth century' becomes 'Was the standard … rising or falling?' You might suspect, even before finding anything out, that some historians argue that the standard was rising, and others have come to the opposite conclusion. It might seem that, in such a recent period of history, there must be an abundance of relevant evidence, including government statistics, which should make it possible to settle the question one way or another. In fact, the evidence is ambiguous and can be looked at in very different ways. There has been a famous debate among historians about this question. What exactly is the evidence on which they disagree? What evidence is used by one side but not the other? Can flaws be found in their reasoning? Have they used large enough samples?

An essay is not a routine information-gathering procedure. It is an intellectual exercise, requiring you to confront unexpected, even surprising, facts, and dig into the sources until you can explain these facts. Robin Winks likened historical research to detective work; every piece of research is a detective story.[1] Before any reading begins, you need to think carefully about the implications of the question, much as did Sherlock Holmes when sitting down with his pipe.

… and proceeds to an answer

What an essay needs to achieve is, purely and simply, an answer to the question it sets itself. No more, no less. Thus, the overriding standard for deciding what you need to write as you proceed to each paragraph is *whether it actually contributes to your answer*.

So, an essay is created by building it up systematically from the core answer in its shortest form, not by cutting down from a mass of material found by reading. Start with the shortest, clearest statement of your answer that you can possibly make, and build the essay by surrounding that essential statement with explanation of the evidence required and the reasoning that follows from that evidence. The success of the answer is to be measured strictly in relation to the terms of the question. There is no room for vagueness.

Essay writing is both a craft and an art. As a craft, it is like an engineering problem. An engineer works out how to do something with the minimum material, at the minimum cost, and in the minimum time, but still to supply what is required safely and adequately to serve a purpose. The engineering analogy suggests one way of thinking of the structure of a history essay (perhaps any academic essay): it has to support your answer, taking the stress economically and adequately, like an arch. If any one of the segments of a true arch is omitted from the structure, it collapses. All segments are necessary.

Sometimes, students ask how much of this or that ingredient, such as facts, interpretation, introduction, or background, is required in an essay. As the arch analogy shows, the answer cannot be given by counting words. The answer depends on the structure of the essay as a whole, and it must be: 'enough to bear the weight of your argument and no more'.

What, then, are the components of the arch? Here are the five main elements:

1 *The question itself*: This must be clearly stated and any ambiguities resolved.
2 *An introduction*: What goes into this depends on the question and how you answer it. You may need to explain why the essay question is 'interesting', in the sense discussed above, and the way you choose to answer it. If there are several possible ways of organizing the answer, make clear which you are choosing and why. Also explain what you understand to be the requirements for an adequate answer, and what things (which might otherwise be debatable) can safely be taken as given for the purpose of the essay.
3 *The factual evidence you need*: Describe it in your own words; give full and accurate documentation (normally in footnotes) so that it is publicly verifiable.
4 *The critical assessment of the evidence*: Remember, history is all about debate and conflicting evidence; discuss possible differences of interpretation and the evidence supporting different views. This is where your independent thought is fully engaged. Look for ambiguities,

problems of interpretation, flaws in some historical arguments, or meanings that others have not seen. Above all, display the reasoning that leads to your conclusions.

5 *Your conclusions*: These are to be the best interpretation that can be made of the particular range of sources you have been able to read.

Naturally, these five do not require equal numbers of words, and they are not separate sections of the essay coming one after another. Some may be largely implicit in the way much of your essay is written. But, implicit or explicit (and usually all of them will be explicit in at least some sentences), they must all be there; otherwise your essay's structure will collapse.

Approaching the writing of an essay

Learning history is not passive; it confronts you with a series of problems raised by written sources, each arising from the tension between what you might initially expect and what the evidence seems to show or what some historians have argued. Each problem demands the engagement of your curiosity and your power of critical appraisal. (The analogy with the puzzles confronting Sherlock Holmes deserves to be mentioned again.)

Writing a history essay is the crucible of historical skill. In this book we shall proceed through all its stages: using libraries; analysing sources; note-taking; planning your essay; drafting it; revising it; benefiting from criticism of it. Not all these will receive equal attention, but they are all essential.

The process begins before you open a book. It begins with the thinking you do as soon as you have the question or title, and with the decisions you make about the reading needed.

Read as many sources as possible

A student once handed in an essay saying: 'You'll see that I used only one book as a source for this essay. It was so good I felt I didn't need anything else.' This will not do. It represents the opposite of the approach required by real history. What is real history? Its raw material is the concrete evidence out there in the world waiting to be explored – in libraries, archives, museums, newspaper morgues, dusty muniment rooms, the memories of eyewitnesses, the chippings of long-dead masons in crumbling stone. It is endless; however much you inspect, there might always be something else which will contradict what you have read and make you revise your interpretation.

To engage in historical study of any topic you must explore everything in its context which might help. It bears repeating that the context might include anything in human experience and thus it is infinitely rich; it can never be exhausted. So consult as many sources as possible. The richness of the material you compile comes partly from choosing the best kinds of sources. Focus on original documents, and search out the most suitable modern books and articles strong in information and interpretation.

It also comes partly from the sheer variety of sources, presenting multiple aspects and multiple points of view. What you read in any one book or any two, however detailed, relevant and informative, might need to be supplemented, criticized or rejected in the light of something read in a second or third; you can never tell until you have done the reading. And the more you read, the more sensitive you become to the subtleties of the subject, the better able to tune in to the interesting (because not obvious) issues involved. A successful essay requires reading, reading and more reading. You can never have enough of it.

When you lack time to read a number of books right through, at least try to read the most relevant chapters of a number of different works rather than spending the same amount of time reading just one or two. Historical insight benefits from the ability to relate things found in different sources, manifesting independent thought.

Finding library sources

One skill probably more important in history than in almost anything else is that of finding needed materials in the library. Make yourself familiar with the location of books and articles. Learn the quirks of the cataloguing system, how to find your way around digital databases and the various online resources, the way the reserve system works if there is one, the location of confined reference books, special collections if there are any, oversize books and so on. This sort of knowledge is not needed for any sort of study, but it is especially important in historical study to have it.

The books relevant to historical subjects will not be all in a single area. You will frequently benefit from sources that might be catalogued under almost any subject under the sun – politics, geography, art history, literature, psychology, law: anything at all might contribute to a particular topic of historical study.

Coping with competition in the library

There is no magic solution to this problem, which might be greater than for other disciplines because of the nature of history. You need to be aware of the standard strategies, such as these:

1 Buy books carefully. It is good to own at least a little basic reading for each topic. Certainly, many factors might affect whether you can

realistically be expected to buy many books for a particular subject of study. University bookshops commonly stock recommended titles. Nowadays, finding books to buy can be greatly facilitated by internet resources (such as Amazon.com and Bookfinder.com), and the availability of electronic editions or books available for reading on digital devices (such as Kindle). It is certainly good if possible to build up a personal library. On internet use generally, see Chapter 5.

2 Learn to exploit the library effectively, as suggested in the previous section.

3 Explore shelves for *books not listed* in your tutorial reading lists. The catalogue numbers of listed items will guide you to the locations of other useful works.

4 Become familiar with relevant *journals*. You need to understand the nature and role of learned journals in the literature of scholarship generally; their importance is explained further in Chapter 4. Browse through back numbers. Skim through interesting-looking articles and reviews.

5 Make good use of *general histories* of the country or region you are studying, and *encyclopedias, bibliographies* and other reference books, whether through the internet or library shelves.

6 Find other libraries. If you have access to an interlibrary loan service, exploit it.

7 Seek advice from your teacher without hesitation.

8 For minor assignments relating to week-by-week tutorials, READ WELL IN ADVANCE and avoid competition for printed material. For any sort of essay or written exercise, it is best to do the reading as early as possible.

Historical orienteering

Here is one sort of exercise which, in a gentle and preliminary way, helps to promote enterprising learning and experience in exploiting the library. It requires you to find the answers to certain questions that cannot be answered without doing some browsing and exploring in order to find out how to do things (as opposed to having them explained). By practising the exercise of initiative, one can develop the instinct for historical study.

This sort of exercise might include tasks such as the following:

- browsing through a particular journal and deciding what sort of focus or emphasis it displays, citing examples of articles which illustrate this

- finding a recent journal article and explaining how it presents an answer to a given problem

- reading an article arguing a particular point of view, and then finding in the library an article arguing against this point of view
- tracking down a particular historical document, where the tracking down involves exploring microfiches or microfilm, databases, rare books or old journals kept in special collections and so on
- tracking down a given unattributed quotation from a book, and describing the steps taken to find it.

Such an exercise encourages independent learning. It is not like jogging along a track; it is more like finding one's way across unknown terrain with minimum navigational aids – historical orienteering.

Asking questions as you go

All the time you read, you must be constantly thinking about and refining the questions to which you want the answers. Your studying is an active process. Remember, the paragraphs you read were not designed at every point to answer exactly the question you are asking. Therefore, you will need to probe and assess, picking out what you need and rejecting the rest.

Thinking about the questions to which you want answers starts before you open a book, and continues all the time you are reading. Think ahead and hypothesize about possible answers. It is essentially a matter of trying out *working hypotheses* as you go. When you begin, they may be mere guesses, but as you read they will become more and more refined. You will probably find that some of your ideas seem less and less plausible as you read, or that they become irrelevant in the light of what you discover. Other ideas, previously unsuspected, will, however, suggest themselves, and you can pick them up and work out their implications as you go. In a word, you follow up *constantly branching questions*.

It may be useful at the beginning of a project to note down some of your ideas in the form of a diagram of possible hypotheses, identifying some possible answers and the sort of evidence that might substantiate or disprove them. This will help to sensitize you to the issues. After a little reading, you may want to revise it radically. After some more reading, you may want to revise it radically again.

The beauty of the exercise is that absolutely no advance knowledge of the subject is required – only common sense. No matter how little you know to begin with, you can make guesses and improve them as you read. Here is an example of some active hypothesizing. It is not intended to display any specialized knowledge; it is intended only to show how, without special knowledge, you can make useful guesses and get your mind working.

Identifying questions and possible answers to guide the active reading process: an example

In the case taken below, it is shown how you can think ahead, guessing at the important questions that need to be asked and what forms the answers might take in order to recognize during the reading process what might prove important.

The imaginary question for an essay is: What were the causes of the Indian mutiny/revolt of 1857? The first point to notice in this rather clumsy title is that there must be some ambiguity. Was there a mutiny or a revolt? What is the difference? A mutiny is an uprising by elements of the armed forces against their commanders; a revolt is an uprising against the government, with some popular support. If there is ambiguity about the Indian mutiny/revolt, that may mean that both soldiers and civilians were involved. This will tell us something about the nature of the movement, with implications about its causes.

Was the movement essentially a mutiny or a revolt?

A1: Was it a revolt? If so, perhaps the rebels were chiefly civilians, but the Indian soldiers joined in.

A2: Was it a mutiny? If so, perhaps the soldiers began it, but at least some civilians joined in.

Suppose that after a little reading you find out that the armed uprising began with the soldiers, and civilian involvement quickly followed. How then did it begin? What sorts of answers might you find?

B1: Perhaps the soldiers mutinied because of poor pay and conditions. Evidence to look for: did Indian soldiers have worse conditions than British soldiers? – worse than they had before they became soldiers? – worse than those of Indian soldiers in other armies?

B2: Was it resentment at harsh orders? What sort of harshness? – worse than the orders given to British soldiers? – to Indian soldiers in other armies?

B3: Was it a clash of religions, Christianity against Hinduism? If so, had British and Indians long been in conflict over religion? Were British officers suddenly trying to convert their soldiers to Christianity?

B4: Was it largely a clash of misunderstanding between cultures? What misunderstandings? Did soldiers misunderstand their orders? Did officers misunderstand the cultural sensitivies of their men? If so, why did the problems happen in 1857 and not earlier?

B5: Was it a mixture of factors difficult to unravel? If so, we must decide which were the most important ones making trouble inevitable.

B6: Was it nationalism? If so, what is the evidence that soldiers were beginning to think of India as a single country which ought to be independent? What would count as evidence of this, as distinct from evidence that they were driven by purely local grievances?

These are just some of the questions which can guide your reading. Suppose that you find most of the answers you want; you still have to decide why the civilian population joined in to the extent that it did. Try out some theories:

C1: Perhaps the population had long been strongly anti-British but only when the soldiers mutinied could they act. This would require evidence of widespread disaffection earlier.

C2: Perhaps nationalism was beginning to spread. Indians saw themselves as citizens of an Indian state. Look for evidence of change from people seeing themselves as members of local communities to seeing themselves as citizens of 'India'.

C3: Perhaps the masses were impoverished by colonial rule, experiencing hardship. Or perhaps they merely perceived themselves to be experiencing hardship. In either case, why? What evidence is there of a changing standard of living in the areas where the revolt was supported by civilians?

C4: Perhaps revolt was fuelled not by popular grievances but by the aspirations of Indian rulers who lost power under British rule. How did these dispossessed rulers behave? Were they prime movers of revolt or just carried along by the uprising?

C5: Perhaps elite Indian groups such as aristocrats and landlords lost privileges under British rule and rose in revolt. What privileges had they lost? How did they behave?

C6: Perhaps civilians had no very strong anti-British feelings, but supported what looked like the winning side. Did civilians join in readily in places where soldiers were not in control?

Historians disagree over many of these questions, and favour many different theories. The questions you raise may lead to answers favouring one side or the other in a debate; it is important to be fair to the evidence for and against each theory. The evidence in this case is, indeed, very complex.

Suppose that your reading seems to indicate that the uprising began among soldiers because of various specific local grievances, and rapidly spread when it was supported by traditional elites (rulers, aristocrats, landlords). What sorts of questions might be good ones to move on from there?

D1: What had been going on that tended to multiply the grievances of the soldiers? Was the army becoming too bureaucratic? – underfunded? Was promotion for Indians becoming too slow? (If so, why?) Were there changes in the types of British people entering the officer corps, or in their attitudes or culture?

D2: What underlying processes might have encouraged the disaffection of the elites? – the spread of British rule to more and more territory? – xenophobia? – opposition to Hinduism? – loss of revenue? – the infection of western liberalism?

D3: Why did the uprising not finally succeed? Why did it break out and become quite strong only in certain areas? What was happening in these areas that was different from others?

These are the sorts of questions that should be tried out in the course of reading; they are not supposed to lead infallibly to a known correct answer. It is to be expected that theories will constantly turn out to be oversimplified. People's behaviour frequently violates the predictions of broad generalizations, such as that the Indians were more unruly than other people, or the British more wicked and greedy, or Christianity and Hinduism always in conflict, or elite people naturally selfish.

In fact, people generally seem to be ready to put up with a great deal of hardship, however defined; what makes them eventually become angry is perhaps most often the result of comparing what they have with what they used to have, or expect to have, or what others who used to be like them now have.

Studying history as independent learning

The contents of this chapter challenge an idea that can sometimes develop naturally from the experience of classes in school – that successful study proceeds by a series of *routine exercises* which anybody can perform, given the right materials. For example, you may have been used to receiving a specially prepared topic guide and a short list of easy-to-find sources in the library, and after reading this material it was always easy to write whatever sort of assignment was demanded for marking purposes.

As you move on to higher levels, however, the nature of study itself changes and goes beyond such routine exercises. Serious historical study is quite unlike the things one learns by drill or highly standardized tasks, such as typing or learning to use mechanical or electrical devices. The real learning comes through developing imagination and independence of thought, and these cannot be guaranteed by simply following rules, any more than can writing good poetry. You will find yourself challenged increasingly to develop independent thought, initiative and enterprise.

Questions

1 Imagine that you are required to write an essay under the heading: 'Was Queen Victoria a powerful monarch?' (another appropriate topic could be chosen). Construct a set of constantly branching questions, on the model of the example in this chapter, to guide the planning of the essay.

2 Imagine that you are required to write an essay under the heading: 'Why did Mussolini come to power?' and that you have no list of recommended reading. What steps would you take to make a list of sources to study?

Knowing your Sources

Chapter overview

► For most practical purposes, the sources used for a history essay consist of recorded words.

► Primary sources are the raw material of research – documents written as closely as can be found to the events studied.

► Secondary sources are writings based on the study of primary sources, such as scholarly books and articles.

► Tertiary sources are writings based on the study of secondary sources, such as historical textbooks.

► Whether a source counts as a primary, secondary or other source for your study depends on what its own sources were and on what exactly you wish to study.

► There is a lot of skill involved in interrogating primary sources, finding out about the past from them often by indirect means, like a detective.

► Any sort of source might be useful (including the internet), but you must be aware of possible dangers.

What makes a good history essay? Many things are involved, starting with skill in the critical appraisal of recorded words. The medium of these words may be newspaper, parchment, stone, celluloid film or anything else; but it still consists of recorded words. These are the objects of study, just as music, human behaviour, the structure of organisms, stars and planets, or anything else may be the objects of study in other academic disciplines. The places where the recorded words are found are the historian's *sources*. Some sources need to be read with different purposes and questions in mind from others.

Types of source

Primary sources

A primary source is not just something which the historian reads and finds important. 'Primary source' is a technical term. It means the *raw material* used by the historian as the most original source of evidence available for use. For example, if he is studying the life of medieval monks, his primary sources should include things actually written in medieval times which give information about monks. They are the materials which come closest to the past events studied. Things written in later centuries about medieval monks should not count as primary sources.

Primary sources are usually documents written more or less contemporaneously with the events and situations to which they refer, especially eyewitness accounts. If there are no eyewitness accounts, a second-hand account written after the situation it describes (for example, a newspaper report the day after) may count as a primary source, if it is the most direct available account. For the historian, the primary source is the nearest he can come to the actual events and circumstances of the past.

Historical research needs to concern itself chiefly with primary sources. Student essays need to give more attention to secondary and tertiary sources which are *about* what the primary sources show, but also need to be based on as much primary source material as possible in order to get the feel of historical methods and problems.

Secondary sources

Secondary sources are documents written on the basis of primary sources. A modern book or article written by a historian who used primary sources is a secondary source. Secondary sources are typically books and articles written to make public the results of research using primary sources. These secondary sources normally follow the conventions of academic writing – they seek to prove the reasonableness of their conclusions by reasoning from evidence that is fully documented so that in principle it can be verified by the reader.

A book based on research is normally counted as a *monograph* – a work concentrating on a single topic, as distinct from a book which surveys a whole field. The term may also designate a work published in a single volume (or perhaps a small number of volumes), as distinct from a journal or other serial publication.

Learned journals constitute an important category of secondary source, and you need to understand the importance of journals in scholarship. Scholarly research might involve either short-term or long-term research. Long-term research is typically designed to lead to the publication of a book. Shorter projects are intended to result in article-length essays published without too much delay; they are often submitted to journals for publication, although the cumbersome processes of peer review and editing can add years to their production. Journals are run by teams of academics and sponsored by academic associations, universities or publishing houses; they seek to build reputations for scholarly quality. Some of the articles in journals make good student reading because they are addressed to specific topics relevant to the subjects of student essays. Others may not, if they are written with a narrow expert readership in mind and take a great deal for granted. You may not find it easy to discover which articles may be good introductory reading, but should take whatever advice you can get.

Well-reputed journals are normally *refereed* – articles published in them are sent for review by expert outsiders before being accepted. There are exceptions; in some fields, and in some countries, scholarly articles by reputed scholars may be sent to, or solicited by, non-refereed journals.

Research-based articles appear not only in journals but also in *edited volumes* – collections of articles, usually on a particular theme. Typically, an editor or editors will arrange for contributions to be submitted by the authors and take reasonable steps to ensure that they fit well together, before sending them out for peer review. Edited collections often consist of articles previously presented as papers at a particular conference; others are brought together in honour of particular eminent scholars, or of dead ones in commemoration of their lives' work.

Tertiary sources

What is secondary is based on what is primary. What is tertiary is based on what is secondary and so on (quarternary, quinary ...). Writings may be based on writings which are based on writings and so on, indefinitely. Tertiary sources are the third in the list starting with primary. They are documents written on the basis of secondary sources. They include student essays, much historical journalism (magazine articles and so on), academic articles in which the authors offer personal views or survey broad fields, published lectures and speeches, and textbooks.

Not all these follow the conventions of academic writing in the sense of providing full documentation (although student essays certainly must). For example, *textbooks*, the purpose of which is to provide introductions to or general surveys of a topic, are a special case, discussed further below.

Ambiguities of classification

Primary sources need close examination as evidence; secondary sources can often be treated as authority but must be read critically; textbooks are useful for introductory reading but not to be imitated in style. But, in some ways, this simple summary must be qualified.

A document may count as primary for one purpose, secondary for another. Edward Said's book *Orientalism* is a study of western writings about Arab countries. These writings are mostly secondary sources for the study of Arab countries, but Said's interest is in what the western writings show about their authors' western culture, and for this they are primary sources.

Even within one book, there may be different sorts of material for the purpose of one sort of study. C.P. Fitzgerald's *The Birth of Communist China* contains passages based on his own direct observation within China earlier in the twentieth century (thus primary sources for the study of twentieth-century China), passages based on his reading of contemporary Chinese newspapers and other documents (secondary), and passages based on his study of writings by other scholars (tertiary).

History textbooks are often substantially based on secondary sources and therefore count as tertiary. However, parts of a textbook are likely to deal with topics on which the author has conducted original research, examining primary sources; such parts are to be considered secondary rather than tertiary. If the author bases most of the textbook on his own research, then most of it is a secondary source.

These examples show that what makes a document count as primary, secondary or tertiary depends on *its relationship to your purpose in using it.* This is important to keep in mind. What makes something a primary source for your essay is the fact that it is direct evidence, belonging to the place and time you are studying. What makes something a secondary source for your essay is that it was written by somebody who used primary sources, and contains discussions of questions useful to examine for help in answering your own question. What makes something a tertiary source is that it also contains material on the topic of your essay, and was written chiefly on the basis of the secondary sources. Everything is relative to the topic and your interest in it.

Exploiting primary sources

Your essay's treatment of primary sources needs to be different from its treatment of secondary or other sources. Scrutinize the primary sources like a detective looking for clues; they are *evidence.* But when you refer in the essay to secondary (or other) sources, you treat them as *authorities.* Basically, this means that when there is no reason to doubt what authorities say, you can accept their judgments and mention them in support of what you write. However, when their claims might be disputed, you should refer to the different interpretations and discuss them.

The statements of primary sources may be practically as truthful (or sincere) as those of secondary sources. A statement in a seventeenth-century official proclamation that the king was beheaded may, after analysis, turn out to be absolutely true, and is evidence of exactly what it says.

But much of the information sought by the historian is less direct, consisting of *what can be inferred from the fact that the words were written*. Take a parish record of the burial of a dead infant. It is direct evidence of the fact that a certain infant had died and was buried in the parish. However, if there were numerous infant deaths in that same year, you can then infer, even without any document saying so, that possibly there was an epidemic of some disease in that year.

This illustrates the detective work that the historian must engage in all the time. Different explanations of the evidence you find should be considered. High mortality could be an index of famine. The historian will wish to look at the geographical distribution of deaths in the year or years when they were abnormally frequent. Disease tends to spread over large areas in the absence of effective medicines or good remedies, but famine may be surprisingly localized.

In England before the Industrial Revolution, parish records rarely showed presumed causes of people's deaths, and to understand the impact of different factors such as disease and famine on the population, the historian must scour a variety of sources and compare different areas.[1] Thus, when you can use primary sources such as parish records, you gain familiarity with the raw material of the historian's trade, and practise your detective skills. This experience familiarizes you with the practice of *asking historical questions* of your sources.

Some historical questions

1 What type of document is it? A statement made to police, a newspaper report, a diary entry, a book of memoirs and a letter to the writer's wife may all describe the same event, but what each can teach us about the past may depend a lot on the type of document it is.
2 Who wrote it? An account by a king claiming a victory might differ strongly from an account written by another party.
3 When was it written? Perhaps what it says was influenced by major issues when the author was writing. Also, its value may be affected by the lapse of time between what it describes and the occasion of its writing.
4 Why was it written? Consider possible motives. Buddhists described the ancient Indian king Asoka as an evil man before his conversion to Buddhism, a saintly man afterwards. Perhaps the motive was to demonstrate the force of Buddhism; perhaps there was no decisive 'conversion' at all.
5 What were the writer's qualifications for writing? How did he obtain his information? Was he in a good position to report accurately?

6 What does the writer insist on? If he insists on some proposition, this suggests that the proposition was denied by some people.
7 What does he take for granted? If something is just assumed to be true, we might suppose that it was not very widely denied.

Exploiting secondary and tertiary sources

Use primary sources as much as possible, but in practice a history essay depends a lot on modern writings by scholars, secondary and tertiary. These are sources which can be referred to as 'authorities', meaning that they are by people qualified to help readers understand the topics on which they write. How should you read these authorities?

Probing the sources

Each work has its own character. Here are some of the questions about a source's characteristics that you need to be able to answer, as a matter of automatic routine:

- When and for what purpose was it written? Check the date of first publication. This may reveal, for example, that certain more recent research findings were not available to the author; or it may give a clue to the intellectual fashions that affected the author's attitudes.
- Does the author disagree with other people who have written about the same subject? If there is a controversy, on which side is he? What is his 'angle'? Whether or not he seems to be on the right side, you may benefit from understanding his point of view.
- How does he use his evidence? What conventions does he follow in presenting it? How detailed and concrete is it? Are his generalizations adequately supported?

Textbooks

History textbooks are broad surveys of topics, regions or countries covering substantial periods of time; their subject matter is commonly too extensive for their authors to have conducted original research on much of it. They are designed largely as introductory reading; unlike research-based publications, they are not required to offer documentation for all their assertions. Their purpose is simply to assist people unfamiliar with a subject to find out about it. (That sort of history book, summarizing the history of a particular area, is a textbook in a different sense from that which applies to a study manual such as this book.)

In the case of history, the nature of the discipline means that anything written by a practising historian about a slice of history may be interesting to his peers. This is because every level of study is characterized by debate and conflicting evidence; it is not possible to write history in a scholarly way about any period or place without identifying problems of interpretation, choosing among possible perspectives, or deciding what to say about gaps in the evidence. So history textbooks are often written by well-regarded historians, and they may often be cited as authorities in the scholarly literature. For example, the French historian George Coedès wrote a major account of the historical knowledge of ancient Southeast Asia; it was published in 1948, and a revised edition appeared in 1964. It incorporated quite a lot of the author's pioneering research using sources that were difficult to access and written in multiple languages, and, although in the course of time the research of others cast doubt on various of his conclusions, his book continued to be cited for the rest of the century.

In some ways, textbooks can be self-indulgent. They can make highly interpretative statements without having to prove them as far as possible. However, they should make clear what points are controversial and debated, and refer to alternative views. An author is encouraged to do this by the knowledge that he will be condemned by his specialist colleagues if his book is merely a trumpet for his own theories.

Therefore, although a textbook and a student essay are both tertiary documents, they are different. What is acceptable in a textbook may not be acceptable in a student essay.

Consider this passage about Dutch colonial administration in the East Indies from D.G.E. Hall's *History of South East Asia* (London, 1964), p. 705:

> So, once more, after a tremendous outpouring of noble sentiment, a programme of 'decentralization' and native welfare was set in motion, with the same almost incredible hesitation that had marked the abandonment of the Culture System. 'Decentralization' was the new gospel.

Notice that it is highly interpretative, and there is no documentation (no footnotes). The author's attitude is shown by his choice of words, suggesting that the Dutch were not very good at matching decisive action to rhetoric. We might wonder whether the author is influenced by an anti-Dutch sentiment that may distort his treatment of the Dutch colonial record (as compared to some others – the British, perhaps).

Nevertheless, we must remember that the book is a textbook. The author is entitled to express these or any other views, so long as he manages to do justice somewhere in the chapter to the arguments for other possible points of view – acknowledging the difficulties confronting Dutch officials in applying colonial policies, for example. A textbook author must be able to put something of himself into his book, for that is what gives it its style, its readability and even its vision.

A textbook can violate many of the principles offered in this book. A student essay, by contrast, must follow the rules, presenting verifiable evidence wherever appropriate. Textbooks are not a model to follow.

First and last things to read

These, then, are the types of source you will confront. How is it best to plan your reading? Often, primary sources are best left to the end, by which time you will know what to look for in them, understand what they say, and be able to obtain maximum value from them. Start with sources written for beginners, and then move on to more specialized works. If you have been able to buy useful books, you may find in them at least a few useful pages of introductory material.

Move from the general to the particular; often this means moving from the tertiary to the secondary and then to the primary. In the preliminary reading phase, look at textbooks, encyclopedias, and general or survey books such as histories of countries, long periods, or major themes. Even a few pages from a general textbook may give you the right orientation to your subject, identifying problem areas and explaining the special terms and categories. Occasionally, a journal article can be good introductory reading if it sums up a topic or problem well, without presupposing much prior knowledge; it is good if you can obtain in advance guidance about which articles might be of this sort.

This preliminary phase lasts only as long as it takes to build up a sense of the issues involved and know the main outlines of the topic. One article or chapter may sometimes have to be enough. Then, in the substantial reading phase, cover as much as possible of the really important sources.

It is while you are reading these works that the topic will take shape for you, underlining the problems, opening up questions, revealing unexpected aspects of the past, and identifying disputes where you find yourself tempted to take sides. Do not forget while reading that there is an essay to write, and at every point judgments must be made about the value of what you read; your critical faculties must be fully engaged.

Questions

1 Think of an essay topic relevant to your course of study for which the main sources would *not* be in the form of recorded words. Make a preliminary search to see what sorts of sources for the topic are available for you to study.

2 What sorts of primary sources might be available anywhere for the study of the following: the life of Hernando Cortés; Viking sea raiders; church architecture in France; the Klondike gold rush?

3 Choose a particular textbook you have used (e.g. a history of a particular country); what, in your experience, are its merits and shortcomings as a study tool?

Using Online Sources

Chapter overview

► As a source for history study, the internet has specific values and limits which must be understood.

► In the digital age, a substantial and growing range of computer-accessible materials is available.

► It is valuable to become familiar with all the digital resources offered by your library.

► Browsing, if intelligently conducted, has its rewards.

► Learn to recognize websites that cater for rigorous scholarly enquiry.

The internet: its value and limits

Internet sources are a special category of source material. In recent years, people have been spending more and more of their time looking at internet sources for all sorts of purposes. Their use in serious historical study requires the utmost care and discrimination. Above all, the fact that they are so easy to use carries with it an often unseen danger.

An essay requires you to consult discriminatingly the best sources available to you and to display independent thought about them. This involves immersing yourself in problems of debate and conflicting evidence, and studying the most useful books and articles. Many of these may not be available digitally, especially because they are likely to have been written quite recently and be protected by copyright. If you attempt to write an essay by relying only on what is turned up by an internet search, you will almost certainly fail to identify all or most of the best sources available, many of which must be found on library shelves, and what you write will not succeed in engaging with the problems of interpretation and conflicting evidence that it should address.

Some history teachers distrust the internet on principle. This principle has some merit: the habit of using the internet as a preferred resource can take up time that ought to be spent finding and reading the best available sources; also, habitual dependence on the internet can encourage the assumption that any publicly accessible material is good to use, and one writer's opinion is as good as any other's. Actually, some writers' opinions are a waste of everybody's time. Seek guidance on what is worth reading. (This guidance should identify sources representing different points of view wherever there is legitimate scholarly disagreement.)

Things written on websites do not have to be written on the basis of primary or secondary historical sources. They might be based on anything whatsoever, and written for any purpose whatsoever, not just to present evidence and debate. You do not know, just from the fact that they are there on the internet, that they have any value at all. *You cannot trust them until you know more about them.*

On the other hand, if you use the internet with due care and discrimination, you may well find in it many useful sources that supply you with information and ideas that would have been hard to come by in the days before the computer revolution. It is desirable to benefit from digital sources as far as possible, and for this reason this chapter is devoted to internet use.

Use the internet discriminatingly

Every year, more and more good sites appear, offering translations, documents, collections of extracts and articles useful for students' purposes, as well as copyright-free reproductions of important lectures and even books.

You should not shun the internet, but should use it discriminatingly, searching out material that can be treated as authority or as authentic source material. There are now many websites providing access to valuable material. But wherever an internet site not specifically recommended for student reading is used in an essay, the annotation to the bibliography should make clear the reasons for regarding that site as an authority, commenting on the academic credentials of the writer or the organization responsible for the site. This chapter is chiefly concerned to offer guidelines for the discriminating use of such resources.

Use common sense to recognize the sorts of writing that do not deserve your attention. They generally lack proper verifiable evidence and do not pay enough attention to different interpretations, to 'debate and conflicting evidence'. Frequently, they suffer from woolly-mindedness or even bigotry. On the recognition of untrustworthy sources, see particularly 'Tendentious or disputatious language' in Chapter 6.

Computer resources in general

Nowadays, it is normal to prosecute study or research in any subject by consulting digital materials, primarily text or images. The range of computer-based study resources is impressive:

- Typically, you can use a computer terminal or other digital device to explore the library of the institution at which you study, and from the same vantage point you can explore the contents of other libraries all over the world, giving you an enormous quantity of material from which to construct a bibliography of resources for any object of study.

- Within your own institution's library, you can probably roam at will through the databases it has acquired, exploring special collections of material on a wide range of subjects.

- Online journals often appear as alternative versions of established printed journals, sometimes a few years in arrears, and obviously are appropriate for student use. Academic libraries nowadays subscribe to digital editions of journals as well as many online reference works.

- Further, you can use the internet, either in the library or sitting at home, to exploit websites that will provide you with filtered and analysed parcels of information about all manner of books, articles and images relevant to precisely defined topics – not just basic catalogue information but also whole reviews, previews enabling you to look briefly inside books, and the page contexts for particular names, terms or phrases.

- And all this is not to mention the range of whole books and articles that can be downloaded and read from the screen in front of you, whether from services that are free to anybody anywhere, paid for by your library and made available to you free of charge, or available for you to read anywhere when you pay to have an account with the provider.

The libraries of tertiary institutions can give students access to a far greater range of sources than in earlier generations, and there is much to be gained by taking advantage of every opportunity to explore the varieties of digital resources you can exploit through membership of such a library. A digital catalogue search is a sort of magic carpet that can take you anywhere. The items included are not only the names of printed books and journals – your catalogue may list all the articles in many of these journals, and if they are not physically present in the library, these articles can be summoned to your monitor screen from a source somewhere else.

Examples of subscription sites

Many digital services useful for historical study are designed for library accounts and can be fully exploited only by paying substantial subscriptions. Websites such as these may give access not only to journals but also to numerous large reference books with online editions, and various services which supply books, articles, documents and special collections of material to libraries. Here are just a few examples of the many digital resources which may be available to you through your library's catalogue:

- *Journal Storage* (JSTOR): www.jstor.org
  Established in 1995 through initiatives in Princeton University, this site has become a major source of digital material, principally runs of journals but also including books and primary sources. By agreement with the publishers of learned journals, issues are fully digitized, and subscribing libraries can make available to their members the contents of all issues, although usually only up to three to five years before the present; for recent numbers, printed copies must be used.

- *Cambridge Books Online*: http://ebooks.cambridge.org
  This is a service providing books to libraries in digital form. Cambridge University Press is prominent in the field of history, and many of its published books are made available as 'e-books'.

- *A Dictionary of World History* (OUP): www.oxfordreference.com
  If your library subscribes to this, you can enter search terms to call up brief factual accounts of historical figures, places, events, ideas and so on. The information you gain is brief and basic, but you will know that it is vouched for by a reputable source.

- *Historical Abstracts*: www.ebscohost.com
  This offers information from bibliographical records collected from learned journals, books and magazines, with coverage of articles dating back to 1953. The articles are drawn from more than 2,600 journals, and access is available to the full text of more than 500 journals.

Generic browsing facilities

Quite apart from the subscription sites, there is a wide range of easily accessible routes to historical information and ideas. Your favoured search engine can be used as a tool of historical enquiry. Skill is involved: you need to enter search terms likely to filter the sort of information you need. You may benefit from including words identifying the topic as a whole and one or two important words, such as names of people or places, which must appear in any useful source.

Your searches will very often summon up, near the top of the list, a relevant entry in *Wikipedia*. This, as is well known, is an encyclopedia of a special sort; the entries in it are composed by any members of the public who take the trouble. Part of the purpose of this institution is that members of the public should be free to communicate the thoughts and knowledge of ordinary people without vested interests, independently of any superstructure of established writers, journalists and publishers. Editors, who, in the nature of the case, cannot be expert in whatever topic appears, do their best to tidy up, but it is a matter of chance how good the content will be. You can reasonably hope that the topic of an entry will be written about quite succinctly by somebody at least fairly knowledgeable, and this makes the work useful as a source of first resort that can be used quickly to assemble mostly accurate factual information. However, for academic purposes, this information must be confirmed and nuanced by your further study. To some extent, it is like most of what you find written on internet sites by authors whose credentials are unknown or obscure to you; without well-informed advice, you cannot know whether any particular article belongs in the category of 'best available sources' for your study.

A potentially valuable instrument in the quest for online sources is provided by the *Google Scholar* site (www.scholar.google.com), which represents a massive attempt to provide access to information of value to scholars, although much of it is essentially bibliographic. Since 2004, it has collected information from peer-reviewed journals and scholarly books appearing online and published by scholarly institutions in Europe and America. A search for any given topic will yield, typically, a great array of citations of books and journal articles and a number of opportunities to read full articles in pdf format; there will also be previews, showing first pages of content, and options to buy directly particular articles or other publications.

A list of possibly useful websites

Various websites offer services helpful in historical study. They include union catalogues and analytical bibliographies, reviews of books, information about books (including extracts, previews and quotations), articles, sometimes whole books, extracts from primary sources or whole documents, lectures, visual images of all sorts, and much else besides. The sites that provide such services do not fall into neat separate compartments, as many of them provide overlapping sets of content; some of them are especially useful for one purpose, others for different purposes. Below are some notes on a few of the sites that are useful for historical study.

- *Google Books*: https://books.google.com
  This exploits information from over 30 million titles (as counted in 2013), assembled from books and magazines compiled from the resources of many publishers and authors and from libraries working as project partners. Search terms selected will produce a list of relevant books; free full viewing will be made available in the cases of works in the public domain, free of copyright restrictions. (This does not include most recent publications.) What appears on the screen will often consist of images from a page of a library copy, sometimes slightly marred by stains or scribbles. Books not available for full view may be represented by 'previews' containing a limited number of early pages (which cannot be duplicated or printed), or 'snippets' of text which contain the words of the search terms. Full-page text no longer includes page numbers, which prevents you from using the website alone to make fully documented quotations in your essays, without going to the trouble of consulting the original books.

- *The Library of Congress digital collections*: www.loc.gov/library/libarch-digital.html
  The Library of Congress has collected material since 1994; the collection includes many rare documentary sources. There are many documents relating to American history and culture, historic newspapers, prints and photographs, and archived websites on specific topics.

- *Digital History*: www.digitalhistory.uh.edu
  A useful set of resources for American history laid out in easily searchable categories, this is rich in material, with detailed textbook-style summaries of topics and events. It divides American history into 20 periods and provides a range of resources for each, including primary sources and images.

- The British Library's *Help for researchers:* www.bl.uk/reshelp/findhelprestype/webres
  Under the heading 'Web resources available to all', many categories of material are accessible – digitized manuscripts collected from internet sources, dissertations, genealogical links and newspaper links, among others. The collection called 'History' includes sections on British History, 'Connected Histories' (which contains sources for British history between 1500 and 1900), the Domesday Book, and much more. Many primary sources are directly accessible.

- *The European Library:* www.theeuropeanlibrary.org/tel4
  This site supports libraries and provides facilities benefiting research throughout Europe; its website gives access to many historical sources

in European languages, including, for example, a big collection of digitized historical newspapers. (The European Newspapers project was established in 2015 and assembled 3.6 million newspapers with nearly 1,000 newspaper titles, drawn from more than twenty European libraries.) The material accessible from this site can be readily searched by description, author, language, year of publication and so on.

- *Gallica*: https://gallica.bnf.fr
  The Bibliothèque nationale de France set up this site in 1997, giving access to materials for French studies, containing (in 2014) half a million books and a large store of images, manuscripts, reviews, periodicals, videos, music scores and other materials.

- *French Revolution Digital Archive* (FRDA): http://frda.stanford.edu
  This archive is a collaboration between the Stanford University Libraries and the Bibliothèque nationale de France. It contains images and digitized text sources of various sorts including parliamentary archives. This collection is dedicated to the provision of materials readily available for research on the period of the French Revolution.

Global and miscellaneous collections

- *WorldCat*: www.worldcat.org
  The Online Computer Center's *WorldCat* catalogue has information drawn from library catalogues in many countries. Over 2,000 million books are covered. An unusual feature is that when you identify a particular book, you can learn which library possessing a copy of it is nearest to where you are.

- *HathiTrust*: www.hathitrust.org
  HathiTrust was established by the University of Michigan, the University of California and the 13 Universities of the Committee on Institutional Cooperation. It draws on the resources of more than sixty libraries in North America and Europe. In 2013 the site gave access to over 10 million volumes, more than 2.7 million of which are in the public domain. You can gain access either to the catalogue record of an item, or to full view; it is often best to search through the catalogue of the particular library storing the book you wish to inspect.

- *Internet Archive*: www.archive.org
  This site is a library of digital material dedicated to 'universal access to all knowledge' and based in San Francisco. Established in 1996, it gives access to published books in digital edition (e-books), miscellaneous texts, web software, film and other materials. Content is acquired from internet sites by web crawlers and a big book digitization project, producing up to a thousand books a day.

- *H-Net – Humanities and Social Sciences Online*: networks.h-net.org
  H-Net is an organization of scholars from various countries and
  disciplines dedicated to maximizing the potential of the internet and the
  World Wide Web for scholarly purposes. Historical studies are prominent
  among its concerns. From the core site, one may find general
  information about the activities and resources of the organization; these
  include discussions, forums, seminars, lectures, tables of contents of
  recent journal issues, news about scholars and scholarship in the
  humanities and social sciences, and general exchange of news and
  ideas.

  From this site you may also follow links to any of the affiliated
  h-networks, which are largely autonomous and provide information and
  services for scholars concerned with particular regions of study or fields
  of research. There are h-networks for history and studies related to
  many countries and regions; the topical or thematic networks are
  concerned with Art and Art History, Colonial and Post-Colonial studies,
  Modern History, Economics and many others; networks are being added
  all the time. The range of miscellaneous discussion forums, lectures and
  events that occupy the networks are largely of interest to practising or
  seriously intending scholars, but for students, the review site
  (networks.h-net.org/browse/reviews) may prove a useful source of
  material, and the rest may, on occasion, be interesting to browse.

- *Records of proceedings in legislatures*
  Records of proceedings of national legislative assemblies are available
  online over periods often extending well into the past, although not in
  unbroken series. For many countries, there exists in print a huge array of
  official records (statutes, committee proceedings, House debates etc.),
  but online sources from before the 1980s or 1990s are to be found in
  various special collections and require an often elaborate process of
  familiarization.

  For the British Parliament, see www.parliament.uk. In 1834 a fire
  destroyed all official records, but parliamentary debates, acts of
  parliament and many other records are available in digital form; see
  under 'Digitised Historical Parliamentary Material', where guidance is
  given to a wide range of online sources.

- *Newspapers*
  Newspapers, national and local, have been in existence for centuries;
  newspapers as we know them began in Britain in 1665, and in America
  in 1690. They normally maintain archives extending far back; many
  archives have been digitized. Records are available for *The Times* of
  London from 1785; see www.thetimes.co.uk/tto/archive.

Questions

1 Take a random essay topic about which you have recently written. Choose some words (not necessarily words in the title) which would be good to use as search terms for your browser. Use these words to search the internet. Then look up the first entry on the resulting list which identifies an item in Wikipedia, and the next three entries that follow it. Check each of these four; how useful is each one as a source for your essay? How far do you think you can trust it as a source for historical study?

2 Look up networks.h-net.org. Find a review of a historical book which looks interesting, and read this review, noticing particularly what the reviewer likes and dislikes. Then use the internet to find another review of the same book. Compare the two reviews.

3 Name and describe a website, not listed in this chapter, which you can recommend for historical study. What, in your view, makes it reliable? What are its limitations?

Reading Critically

Chapter overview

► Reading critically means assessing trustworthiness, *not* disagreeing with everything.

► Critical reading of anything involves provisionally accepting its authority only while there is no reason to distrust it, and assessing its value rigorously as soon as any possibility of untrustworthiness appears.

► Everything an author says needs to be considered either as a statement of fact which you can provisionally accept, or as an interpretation, opinion or judgment.

► Prejudice and bias are harmless when we begin studying any topic; they are harmful when they prevent us from looking coolly at the evidence or from being ready to change our minds.

► If an author belongs to some particular class of person, if his language expresses strong adherence to one side in a debate, or if his conclusions are expressed in a strong, uncompromising way, none of this is enough to condemn his conclusions as wrong.

► Tendentious, disputatious language is generally undesirable, but it is more important to assess the actual evidence and reasoning of the argument before we condemn it.

► Balance is shown by readiness to look coolly at the evidence on both sides of a question before reaching a conclusion, not by the character of the conclusion.

It is often said that being 'critical' is essential to effective study and writing. What is this 'criticism'? Reading critically does not mean disagreeing with everything. It means not taking what you read for granted. As you read, think what is significant about every point advanced and why the author makes it. How does it fit into the plan of the chapter? Is it presented as factual evidence, or as a judgment representing the writer's conclusions? Has the writer given good enough evidence for his judgments?

Reading for information and reading for ideas

Here are two approaches to historical reading. Both are needed; what matters is knowing which you need at each point.

One is to learn specific facts or details. Books about study methods often advise on the advantages of skimming, scanning and skilful use of the index and table of contents. Such techniques are useful when you are acquiring information about a topic – identifying important chapters, finding where particular people, places and events are mentioned, and learning to run your eyes quickly down each page, instantly recognizing what is useful or not useful.

The other is to assess the whole text, relating it to its context and understanding the author's ideas and purposes. Why is a particular historian arguing as he does? Is he taking sides in a particular debate? (If so, knowing it helps you to understand his thinking better.) How specific is his evidence? How well documented is it? Where does he differ from other historians?

With this sort of critical reading, what matters is not so much the number of facts or ideas you can take in per hour as the depth of understanding you gain as you read. It is better to spend days over a book and see what the author is really trying to do than to spend an hour and achieve only a page of information just as easily discoverable from an encyclopedia.

Both these approaches are needed at different times.

The problem of authority

You need to combine two different attitudes to the sources: criticizing, and accepting authority. These may seem inconsistent. How can they be reconciled?

Basically, everything should be read critically. Suspicion should become a natural attitude whenever you pick up a book or, especially, a website. Keep questions in mind. Why are you reading it? What were the writer's motives, qualifications, values? How long ago did he write? How close was he to the events he describes? Is the publisher a reputable academic house?

More questions than these are needed to screen out unreliable sources. It is possible for even the most untrustworthy of books or websites to have the outward trappings of scholarly argument – they are written by people titled 'Doctor', they have footnotes and bibliographies, and they quote evidence aplenty, but the evidence is selected wholly to suit a predetermined argument, and its logic is twisted. You must be able to detect this. What you read does not necessarily deserve to be treated as authority.

The acceptance of authority in the absence of reasons for rejecting it

Nevertheless, you are not expected to argue about *everything* you read. Your authorities, if they are professional historians writing recently, probably know what they are doing, and you should accept their authority *until you have a reason for questioning and discussing it.*

Use common sense. Accept a source's authority for something if there is no apparent reason to question it – if, for example, it is based on documented evidence, is written by a historian, is based on research, is fairly up to date, looks reasonable, does not conflict with anything else you have read, and seems unbiased.

It would be pointless to criticize statements by established historians when you have no sensible criticism. The following paragraph deliberately caricatures how a student might take too literally the recommendation to show independent thought (it is an imaginary case, but illustrates a real danger):

> Acton alleges that William the Conqueror invaded England in 1066. This may be true, but he gives no footnote for it, and I have been unable to make any independent assessment of his evidence. It is true that other historians such as Smith[1] and Jones[2] mention the same thing, but they were writing later than Acton, and were perhaps uncritically repeating what Acton had said. We need to take into account the possibility that Acton was biased. Perhaps his family was of partly Norman descent. At all events, we should not accept claims like this without better evidence than he has given us.

Here, then, we have a fairly extreme example of overcritical writing. At the opposite extreme would be an uncritical statement like

> The assassination of President J.F. Kennedy in 1963 was the work of elements within the CIA.[1]

In this imaginary case, the essay makes a questionable claim – it contradicts what most people think – and supports it by referring in the footnote to some source. Even if we suppose that the source actually supports the claim, this does not justify the way it is expressed in the text. It is obviously questionable, so should not be expressed as if it were factual evidence.

These are extremes; the line between a statement safe to treat as factual evidence and a claim liable to be disputed by others is not always easy to draw.

Distinguishing between factual evidence and judgment or opinion

There are clues showing the teacher how well an essay writer understands what is required in an essay. One lies in how well an essay distinguishes between statements in sources that deserve to be treated as factual evidence, and statements that present judgments or opinions *about* the evidence. You need to be able to make this distinction clearly.

What you can treat as factual evidence consists of the factual statements made by your authorities which you have no reason to distrust. If a statement looks questionable, or another historian contradicts it, or it is difficult to see what good reason the author has for making it, then you should not treat it as fact. Even if actually correct, it represents inference, judgment or interpretation rather than straightforward fact. Do not take a claim on trust in any of these conditions.

The distinction between fact and opinion is to be shown by presenting statements of factual evidence in your own words and footnoting them, and by identifying statements of inference as what they are. Signal them by the appropriate words: 'Hobsbawm argues that ...', 'In Hill's view ...', 'According to Acton ...'. You then succeed in showing that you have not been reading Howbsbawm, Hill or Acton naively and uncritically, noting their words as gospel truth.

Fact and opinion: an example

Imagine that you are preparing an essay on the collapse of the ancient civilization of the Indus Valley. In a book, you read: 'The city did not just wither away – it was abandoned suddenly.' You might possibly accept it as a fact. It looks like useful evidence: the sudden abandonment of a city suggests that some single event like invasion by nomads contributed to the collapse of the civilization. However, critical reading requires you to ask: how does the author know this? What is the evidence?

If your authority is a textbook, it may not have any documentation. Very well; so long as you have no reason to distrust the textbook, you are entitled to use it as an authority. If no ground for distrust appears, you may want to treat this statement as factual after all. But not necessarily. Suppose it was written quite a long time ago and your other reading has shown that the archaeology of the area has progressed greatly since. In this case, it seems unwise to trust the book. It is always unsatisfactory to depend on an unsupported statement. You want better evidence.

Suppose that you find exactly the same statement in a secondary source, with footnotes referring to articles in archaeological journals. To develop the argument that the city was abandoned as a result of invasions, you will wish to consult these articles and find the actual evidence. Suppose that the journals are not available; at least, with a documented claim in a research-based source, you have found a better source than the original textbook.

But you really want an explanation of this claim that the city was abandoned suddenly. Suppose you find it in another book: five skeletons were found in the upper levels of the excavation of the city, showing that they had been left sprawling on the ground. This looks like solid factual evidence. In inhabited cities, dead bodies are not left sprawling where they fell; something is done with them. So the skeletons suggest sudden abandonment, possibly invasion. You can use this statement as factual evidence so long as you find no reason to distrust it.

But now suppose that, in a more recent book, you find the claim that the excavation of the site was not very rigorously conducted, and that, after a re-examination of the evidence, it appears that the skeletons were not actually at a level corresponding to the moment of the end of the city. They might be the bodies of nomads at an abandoned campsite left there well *after* the city had become uninhabited and left to fall into ruin. This instantly alters the case. The new interpretation could still be wrong – you must try to assess the evidence on both sides – but you can no longer treat the first archaeologist's claim about the skeletons as a statement of factual evidence.

You must treat critically every claim you meet. Any historical statement *might*, in some unpredictable way, turn out to be false or debatable – even the claim that William the Conqueror invaded England in 1066. There is no clear and absolute line dividing statements of fact from statements of inference, judgment or opinion.

Nevertheless, in the light of all your reading, you must decide what you can treat as statements of factual evidence for the purpose of your essay. These are generally the best documented statements in the sources where the relevant arguments are explained in the most detail, and they are all statements which, so far as you are aware, there is no reason to distrust. These statements you may treat as fact without discussion; refer to the evidence, and in footnotes cite sources in required detail.

Other statements must generally be treated as expressions of *opinion, judgment* or *inference.* Identify them as judgments open to debate ('Smith argues that ...', etc.). This is an important distinction; if you refer to an obviously debatable statement as if it were factual evidence, you instantly give the impression that you cannot tell the difference.

The examples below show the two different ways of treating the statements you wish to use from your sources, one as a statement of fact (because you see no reason to distrust it), and the other as a claim that somebody has made (but which might be open to challenge):

> *Example 1:* Five skeletons were found sprawled in an open space at the top level of the excavation, indicating sudden abandonment of the city.[1]

> 1.   J. Smith, *The End of the Indus Valley Civilization*, New York, 1990, p. 100.

> *Example 2:* Smith claims that five skeletons, dating from the moment of the city's abandonment, were found sprawled in an open space at the top level of the excavation,[1] although Brown, who has re-examined the evidence, suggests that ...

> 1.   J. Smith, *The End of the Indus Valley Civilization*, New York, 1990, p. 100.

All this shows why it pays to *read as widely as possible*. Suppose that you were to base your essay essentially on the disputed interpretation of those five skeletons. The more authorities you consult, the safer you are.

You need to read with a critical attitude, recognizing the statements that deserve to be treated as factual evidence, and those that must be treated as judgments or opinions. So you need not only to report *what* your sources say, but also to think critically *about* what they say, recognizing statements that might possibly be disputed. Be alert for occasions to apply your critical skill.

Prejudice and bias

Sometimes you may wish to criticize prejudice or bias in your secondary sources, thereby earning credit for independent thought. However, you must be able to see through the superficially obvious qualities of what you read to the actual value of whatever the author is arguing. How might bias or prejudice really damage the value of historical writing?

Prejudice

'Prejudice' means judgment in advance. There is no harm in having a belief about something in advance of studying the evidence. Before starting our investigation, we may often favour one possible conclusion. We are rarely *totally* neutral. If we study the Second World War without ever having read about it before, we may expect that Hitler will turn out from our examination to be wrong, indeed very bad. If this counts as a prejudice, it is natural.

What matters, though, is our readiness to be persuaded by evidence. In the end, the prejudice may indeed be confirmed – but then it will be no longer a prejudice but a considered judgment. A prejudice in the bad sense is one that we are not willing to change through an open-minded enquiry.

Bias

A bias is a built-in tendency to lean to one side, to favour one side. Again, what matters is whether this inclination prevents us from accepting evidence against it.

Do not confuse prejudice or bias with just having an opinion. We all have opinions; what matters is whether we are ready to let our opinions be changed by examining the evidence.

Accept what evidence shows

Life is too short to examine everything exhaustively, and we must admit that many of our beliefs are prejudices picked up uncritically from casual conversation and reading, rather than by rigorous argument. Many people have prejudices in favour of George Washington, democracy, free trade, Montessori schools, Galileo, the Renaissance and Mother Teresa. Many have prejudices against Genghis Khan, King John, fascism, feudalism, Confucian education, Savonarola, the upper classes and Stalin. Some of these prejudices might indeed tend to be confirmed for most people by rigorous scrutiny of the evidence, but others might be overturned. People should be willing to change their minds, and sometimes do.

Any author might approach his research with a prejudice, in this sense. That is only natural. What matters is the fair-mindedness of what follows. Once you understand this, you should be able to recognize when you are entitled to complain about bias in one of your sources and when not.

What bias is and is not

Here are three important cases where a student, enthusiastic to demonstrate an independent critical mind, may condemn what an author says as bias, but where he may have been too hasty.

You might suspect bias in a book:

1 on the strength of who or what the author is
2 on account of tendentious language used by the author – words which look prejudiced, implying a flat denial of some other possible point of view
3 when the conclusions offered seem to lack balance.

Any of these three cases might suggest the *possibility* of bias. They are not, however, the *same thing as bias*; and each of them may indeed be consistent with an otherwise rigorous and scholarly approach. It is necessary to recognize what is bias and what is not.

The author as interested party

Imagine that a book about Napoleon is condemned in an essay because the author is French; a work on economic history is condemned because the author is a Marxist; a work on the Reformation is condemned because the author is a Catholic.

All these criticisms are mistaken. Certainly, you should be alert to whatever facts about the author and his beliefs you can pick up. Knowledge of the author's background and values may sensitize you to his view of the world, and help you to understand his thinking, right or wrong. That is one thing. But it is quite another to declare that, because the author belongs to a certain group and has certain values, his work therefore suffers from a certain sort of bias and cannot be trusted. In assessing what you read, you must keep the two things quite separate.

After all, every research topic has to be approached with some ideas in mind – theories to be put on trial, hunches to be tested. To have an expectation about what the evidence will show is no crime; it is a virtue, for it gives dynamism to the investigation. A detective without any theory about who the murderer might be is not likely to make much progress. What matters is to examine all the evidence fairly.

Tendentious or disputatious language

It is not always easy to decide what sorts of writing can be regarded as reasonably objective and what sorts use language with unwarranted judgments built into them. In a sense, almost any use of words presupposes certain unproved assumptions by the speaker. The very utterance of words presupposes that there exists agreement between speaker and hearer about the meanings of words and the realities of the world they inhabit; sometimes the presupposition may prove false.

The purist can argue that there is no such thing as a statement that is not theory laden. Any judgment *might* be challenged on some ground or other. Consider the innocent-seeming statement: 'William the Conqueror invaded England in 1066 AD.' It looks uncontroversial; yet the choice of words, however innocent-seeming, nevertheless implies judgments which *might* be questionable. For example, the word 'invade' might be said to prejudge the question whether England was foreign territory or not. William thought it was his own territory. One does not 'invade' one's own territory. So the statement might be considered tendentious. Again, the title 'the Conqueror' is not one that William possessed at the time; in bestowing it upon him we are uncritically adopting a judgment made by later generations. Finally, it might be held that the abbreviation 'AD' implies a judgment, which many would dispute, that Jesus really was the Messiah. (There is also the problem that Jesus was actually born in about 6 BC.)

For practical purposes, though, we cannot afford to be excessively pedantic in deciding what we can allow writers to say; ordinary language carries many conventional assumptions which are harmless unless we specifically wish to challenge them. Real tendentiousness appears when a writer deliberately chooses words gratuitously, implying a debatable belief.

Consider first a borderline case:

> The governor was advised that the methods of licensing that he proposed had proved disastrous in Australia, but he persisted with his scheme; the riots that followed could have been avoided if he had acted upon the advice he was given.

This shows the writer's judgment of the governor's action, but it might well occur in a properly presented argument, so long as each claim made is *adequately documented and shown to be a fair factual statement*. We see here how tendentiousness needs to be judged in relation to the context; if facts given in the context justify the choice of words in the expression of the writer's judgment, that is a good defence. On the other hand, a sentence such as

> The governor persisted stubbornly with his ill-advised scheme.

is less defensible. The difference is that, by using the value-laden expressions 'stubbornly' and 'ill-advised scheme', the writer is seeking to influence the reader by the choice of heavily loaded words, rather than by rational argument. It is this that constitutes tendentious, disputatious, polemical or partisan language.

Part of the stock in trade of critical reading is to be able to recognize the use of tendentious language wherever you meet it.

Take an example:

> The union bosses recklessly went ahead with their plan, knowing that they could count on the uncritical support of their indoctrinated flock.

This passage is tendentious. What prejudices it is the choice of words calculated to make the reader accept a judgment without examining the evidence for it. The words used imply disapproval, if not contempt. They attempt to influence the reader, independently of any evidence, simply by the choice of words.

A passage can usually be shown to be couched in prejudicial language if the fact it states can be expressed in other words which do not have any tendency to influence the reader towards the same judgment. They may have a tendency to influence the reader towards a totally different judgment.

Consider this variant of the same passage:

> The union leaders pressed ahead boldly, knowing that their programme of
> extensive consultation and discussion had won their members' loyalty.

Here the same fact is recorded, but in language which is calculated to
influence the reader to a favourable judgment.

Below are some examples of statements, most of which (with one
exception), in different degrees and depending on the context, seek to
sway the reader by the choice of expressions which already imply
judgments:

1 The government had to choose: it could support either recondite art,
   monumentally expensive grand opera and elitist broadcasting that
   would be incomprehensible to most people, or popular cultural
   activities accessible to ordinary working folk.
2 The decision to go to war was in clear violation of all three of the
   treaties described above.
3 This short-sighted policy of allowing the unbridled importation of cheap
   manufactured goods caused incalculable harm to the long-suffering
   population.
4 The well-fed abbot and his burly henchmen gave the hapless townsfolk
   no choice: they had to pay an extortionate feudal levy *as well as* the
   normal church tithe.

Just one of these sentences (you can decide which) suggests disapproval,
but is not really tendentious; it confines itself to reporting apparent facts.

However, it is important to recognize that the culpability of such
writing as these sentences represent varies according to context. There is
no harm, in principle, in a writer expressing any attitude whatsoever; what
matters is the means by which he seeks to influence the reader. It is good
practice to avoid using words which tend to prejudice the reader, but
when a particular judgment is fully justified by the argument that has
gone before – when all the cards are on the table – there may be
comparatively little harm in a statement which lets the reader know how
the author feels.

Consider the example above, in which union leaders are condemned.
Suppose that, on earlier pages of the work in which the passage appears,
hard factual evidence had been offered showing that it should have been
obvious to the union leaders that their proposed action could not bring
about the results they wished for. In such a case, if the author's meaning is
carefully made clear, the use of the word 'reckless' to describe their
conduct might well be justified. So with the other words and phrases
calculated to prejudice the reader towards the author's judgment; if the

judgment is properly argued, the otherwise tendentious-looking phraseology that embodies it may be defensible.

Below are two examples of tendentious language found on the internet. Note, however, that these writers are not writing in scholarly journals and should not be blamed for expressing their views in the way they do; but, if the same things were written in scholarly literature, we might be less charitable. A fully fair judgment would require examination of the whole context, and we would need to decide whether the evidence justifying such expression was present. All that said, the passages in question can be seen to use tendentious language:

> Those familiar with Tamil as well as Sanskrit can see on what pathetic scholarship Thapar's argument regarding *mriga hastin* is concocted.[1]

Here the word 'pathetic' goes well beyond normal scholarly usage to castigate the book under review. Notice also that 'concoct' is far from value free – it is a word used to disparage the methods by which something is put together, suggesting that the ingredients are chosen with an illicit purpose.

The second passage (from an article which had also appeared in a newspaper) is more subtle:

> But our illiberal secularist missionaries cannot tolerate such a choice. They think no children should be taught any alternative to scientism.[2]

'Illiberal secularist missionaries' does not contain any powerfully emotive word or extreme claim, but 'illiberal' clearly implies that those so described lack tolerance and favour arbitrary policies, and 'missionaries' may be used neutrally when it refers to real religious missionaries but in other contexts suggests that the people so described are zealots or fanatics bent on obtaining converts. 'Secularist' can often be used neutrally, but when it is already clear that the author is identifying some group in order to criticize it, the suffix '-ist' insinuates that the people in the group can be pigeon-holed by virtue of some shared belief by which they can be quickly judged. The sentence beginning 'They think …' represents a common device – that of attributing to some group, without discussion, the most extreme of the range of views found among its members. None of this makes the passage extravagantly polemical, but in a relatively subtle way it invites the reader to share an attitude of disdain for what is criticized.

You need to recognize prejudicial or tendentious language when you see it, so that you may avoid being influenced irrationally. This is an important element in clear thinking.

Nevertheless, you must not think that the ability to recognize it puts into your hands an easy-to-use tool that will infallibly enable you to pass judgment on what you read. Judgment requires sensitivity. You must take account of the quality of a whole argument, not judge it just by the ill-chosen words of some sentences. Check whether value-laden words (such as 'reckless') are justified by factual argument already presented. Further, in some sorts of writing, such as textbooks, review articles and reflective essays, the use of tendentious language may be more forgivable than in research-based writing. In a textbook, for example, the writer's slightly quirky point of view may not destroy the book's value as a useful introductory survey of a topic.

However, where the object is to persuade by rigorous argument from evidence, tendentious language should be avoided. The use of coloured phraseology can only distract and hinder in the pursuit of this goal; only when the writer has established his conclusions by cool and rigorous discussion of the evidence is it at all consistent with good practice to express views in judgmental, value-laden terms.

'Balance'

There is another way in which we might be tempted to accuse a historical work of bias: if the author argues strongly for a particular point of view, offering an uncompromising conclusion and giving a straightforward answer to the question without qualification, a student might think that this is evidence of a lack of balance and therefore shows bias. Academic writing, surely, requires balance. But what is balance?

There is a temptation, after studying a topic enough to see its complexity, to use this insight as an all-purpose argument against any proposition advanced by anybody who does not share it. 'It's not like that; the whole matter is much more complex', we may say. Indeed, historical research often tends to blur the edges of clear-cut categories, to reject simple-seeming answers as misconceived, to discover important ambiguities in what at first seems straightforward. This is fair enough. Historical reality is complex. It is good to recognize this; it helps you to tune in to the way historians work, distrusting simple-looking judgments and looking for the variety of factors that affect the answer to a question.

Often enough this is an appropriate response, but it is not automatically and necessarily appropriate, and sometimes it can be taken too far; sometimes straightforward judgments are entirely adequate. It may happen that the only correct answer to the question set is a resounding 'yes' or a resounding 'no'. Perhaps Hitler really was a disaster for Germany; perhaps agriculture in Russia really did suffer under Stalin; perhaps the signing of the Magna Carta really was a turning point (of some sort) in English constitutional history; perhaps the invasions of barbarians (however complex the web of causation may have been) really were a major cause of the collapse of the Roman Empire. Or again, in each case, perhaps not; but it would be folly to rule out the possibility that a straightforward statement can be true. Therefore, an uncompromising conclusion by a historian is not necessarily a sign of a lack of balance. Real balance is shown by a readiness to look coolly at the evidence on both sides of a question before reaching a conclusion, not by the character of the conclusion.

Questions

1 Think of a useful historical book you have read (or read most of) recently. Describe the author's opinion on any debatable topic which is dealt with in the book. Did you find the argument for this opinion convincing? Why, or why not? Have you read any scholarly writing which expresses a different opinion on the same topic? If so, how convincing was it? If not, try to find such a source now. Which source offers the better argument, and why?

2 Consider the ways in which the following sentence seeks to influence the reader to share the writer's opinion:

   The leader of this motley crew was later to acquire the adulation of a naive posterity, a fame which was perhaps best warranted by his one striking achievement: he was able to buy, at the rock-bottom price which was all that his movement's ill-furnished coffers could then afford, a job lot of red shirts for his men to wear.

   How might the same thought be revised to express an opposite view, or a neutral one?

3 Should a historian express strong feelings about the people or affairs he deals with?

Taking Notes

Chapter overview

► Find the system of note-taking that suits you.
► Do not write too many notes.
► Do not copy out sentences verbatim from what you read.
► Copy only sentences you expect to use as quotations.
► Understand why an essay might quote anything.
► Notes should be very easy to read, broken up by headings and subheadings.
► Think ahead to the essay while you read so that you can recognize what is good to note and what is not.
► One piece of advice is so important that it deserves to be repeated here: do not write too many notes!

There are two reasons why this chapter should not be very long. One is that note-taking in historical study is not very different from note-taking in other disciplines, except that there should be more of it to do. The other is that note-taking is, after all, very much a matter of personal taste and experience. Some people use little notebooks, some large sheets; some use note cards (good for breaking your notes into compact and manageable units) and some prefer flimsy airmail sheets (reducing bulk and weight of accumulated notes); some like lined paper and some prefer plain; some (with laudable economy) use the backs of scrap paper, and some like clean crisp pages.

In the end, it does not matter whether you use a polychromatic array of pens or a much-chewed pencil (so long as notes are legible months later), whether you write every word in full in beautiful copperplate or use professional shorthand (but remember that shorthand needs to be read and used soon after it is written), or whether your writing sprawls grandly across the page or needs a microscope for anybody else to read. What is important is simply that you should be able to use your notes for their intended purpose.

Do not write too many notes

Many students find difficulty in knowing what to note down as they read and what to pass by. Quite often, they end up noting practically every fact or idea they meet, making piles of indigestible notes that are difficult to use later. As you read, almost everything looks as though it *may* turn out to be important to you, and you do not want to risk losing it while you have the chance to note it down. But then you may spend six or seven times as long noting a book as you would have spent if you had merely been reading it, understanding it and thinking about how to use it.

There is a dreadful fascination in the note. An inner voice tells you that, if you do not note down an important-looking fact, it will be lost when you want to write the essay or revise for the examination. Resist this fascination. Read purposefully, knowing what sorts of ideas or information you need and what not.

Of course, in your work on a fresh subject, you may need to make fairly dense notes on some sources, particularly when you are reading a chapter or an article known to be full of important basic information about your topic. The first of the two examples of note-taking given at the end of this chapter may qualify in this way. What matters is that you should be able to recognize what sources are rich enough to warrant dense notes.

However, if you are planning to read many sources, it is usually best to lean the other way – when in doubt, leave out. Be prepared to lose a few genuinely important facts or ideas. This may be difficult, but, even if you miss something important in one book, it is likely to appear in another book, and when you meet it again you will have realized why you need it – if you have been thinking questioningly while reading.

Do not copy out verbatim from books

A corollary of not taking too many notes is the following important maxim: except when there is really good reason to do so, *do not copy out verbatim from books*. This is for the following reasons:

1   Copying out is tedious and anti-intellectual. It discourages thought. Always think actively and questioningly while reading. Every note you write should reflect independent thought, analysing, filtering, collating and relating what you find to the question set. If you are thinking actively, you will be able to use your own words effectively, and the act of drafting the note will help to grow the ideas governing your eventual essay or examination answer.

2   Sometimes, sentences from notes find their way unchanged into essays. If such sentences are copied verbatim from books, the practice of copying may lead to inadvertent plagiarism. This must at all costs be avoided.

3   Almost certainly, especially if you are thinking actively, you will be able to express what you want to note in fewer words than the original, thus saving valuable time.

When to write out quotations

Just sometimes, it is worth copying out word for word sentences from what you read. When? Basically, you need to copy only those sentences that you may want to *quote* in an essay.

What sentences are these? This is discussed in Chapter 11, 'Quotations' (pp. 108–9). Briefly: you should not quote something just because it is important, or even because it is well expressed. There is no need to quote anything, generally, unless you wish to *discuss the actual sentences you quote*. Two main cases of this are:

● in primary sources, words which, in themselves, constitute evidence to be discussed

● in secondary sources, words which are *debatable* at points which matter to your argument, especially where you compare one author's judgments with another's.

Commonsense guidelines

The points above enshrine the most important principles. The detail of practice is largely a matter of personal preference. Whatever suits you is what is right. But here are some practical, commonsense guidelines, including the points already made and others besides:

1   *Notes need to be practical for revision purposes,* so must be brief.

2   *Notes should represent your own thinking.* Do not copy out unless you may want to use a quotation.

3   *Put at the beginning all the information about the source which is needed to cite correctly* (author's name, etc. as required by the documentation conventions you are following). Perhaps include the library catalogue number for whenever you might want the book again.

4   *Include page numbers for all points noted.* You will need these for footnotes, or future revision. Page numbers could be tucked into one margin.

5   *Notes should, above all, be easy to take in at a glance,* and easy to navigate. Therefore, they should be *well broken up with headings and subheadings.* Notes are indigestible if they ramble on without break or subheading.

Try to identify points and subtopics as you go, and find ways of signalling the beginning of a new point. Avoid writing more than about three lines without a heading or subheading. Even if the pattern made by your breaks and subheadings does not match well the logic of the text you are noting, it is still better to have a partially analysed text than an unanalysed one represented by a slab of unbroken prose.

6 *Notes should match the purpose for which they are made,* sometimes fairly dense and sometimes fairly sparse. A chapter of general background, most of it familiar from previous reading, may require very few notes or none at all, but still be useful to read. A particular few pages of another book may require very full notes. Never read purposelessly. Good notes reflect purpose and discrimination.

7 *Your notes must be comprehensible to you many months later.* If you cannot read them, something has gone wrong.

8 *Your notes should fit your system.* Look ahead. Eventually, you will have a thick pile of notes; they will be easier to use in the future if you consistently use the same size of paper, supply clear useful headings, and arrange topics in a logical sequence.

9 *Never write anything on the pages of a library book.* Underlining and annotations will not help you once the book is returned, and are most unlikely to help any later reader, who will have different purposes in mind. The more defacement there is in a book, the more the book is ruined. Think of it as a jewel box, containing gems of wisdom.

Note-taking examples

The examples to be offered represent notes taken from part of a book: F. Thistlethwaite, *The Great Experiment: An Introduction to the History of the American People,* Cambridge: Cambridge University Press, 1955, pp. 146f. Read the following passage, from which the notes below are taken:

> In the early years of the Republic, men expected that slavery would die out as indentured service had done. The long decline of tobacco and indigo planting encouraged a shift to mixed farming for which slaves were less profitable. Men of affairs in the South, as in the North, pinned their hopes, not only on the cultivation of varied agricultural arts, but on trade, transport and the establishment of industry. John C. Calhoun voted for the tariff of 1816 and advocated the mercantile expansion of southern Appalachia. Under pressure from Britain the slave trade was abolished in 1807. Humane planters, in the golden afterglow of the Enlightenment, followed Jefferson in manumitting slaves in their wills, and supported the American Colonization Society in its efforts to establish a colony of free Negroes in Liberia.

The advent of King Cotton put an end to such hopes. The cry for raw cotton in Lancashire mills was heard in Carolina; and when in 1793 Whitney's ingenious cotton gin made it possible to separate [p. 147] seed from lint in the short-staple plants which could be grown inland, southerners turned thankfully to this new, bonanza crop to solve their economic ills. After the War of 1812, cotton eclipsed rice, tobacco and sugar as the chief concern of a South which, under this stimulant, spread westwards to Louisiana and beyond to Texas wherever the long, warm growing season permitted. The crop doubled in size each decade, from some seventy thousand bales in 1800 to nearly four million in 1860. Lancashire's insatiable appetite for cotton fastened slavery ever more firmly on the South. Negro slaves provided the best, indeed the only, labour force whereby Europe's need for cotton could be made good from the rich, virgin soils of the interior. Cotton was a simple crop to raise, well suited to Negroes who could endure the heat and heavy toil, and to slave gangs who were most economically employed in the slow, steady rhythm of an unskilled field job.

Before making any notes, first you need to be sure that you understand what you are reading. If there is serious difficulty in following what the writer is saying, you may be better off turning to another source instead.

It is essential to read the passage with a question in mind; otherwise there will be no way of deciding what deserves to be noted down and what not. Here, let us suppose that you are reading this book with a view to writing an essay under the title: 'Why did the number of slaves in America increase in the first half of the nineteenth century?'

	F. Thistlethwaite, *The Great Experiment: An Introduction to the History of the American People,* Cambridge: Cambridge University Press, 1955, pp. 146f.
146	Late 18th cent. Expectation: slavery would die out: for various reasons: • Decline of plantation crops, more mixed farming (not so suitable for slave labour) • With Independence, hopes for commerce, industry, transport in South • Slave trade abolished 1807 • Liberation of slaves by Enlightenment-influenced owners, who made wills releasing slaves, helped freed slaves go to Liberia
146f	Why cotton caught on in South • Enormous demand for cotton from England – 'The cry for raw cotton in Lancashire mills was heard in Carolina' • Adoption of cotton boosted by technology – Whitney's cotton gin 1793 allowed processing of short-staple plant growable inland • Simple crop to raise

147	Why cotton boosted demand for slaves
	• Black slaves 'best, indeed the only' suitable labour force
147	• Well able to endure tough hot conditions of cotton field work
	• Accustomed to repetitive unskilled operations
	• Cheap, easily fed, housed, clothed
	Growth in numbers of slaves
	• 1800: about 1m Africans; 1860: 4.5m; these mostly slaves in South

Points to notice

This is very dense noting; usually you will not need so much detail. However, in this case, there is a lot of information in a small space very relevant to the essay topic. Sometimes, then, dense noting may be appropriate. In this example, dense notes help to illustrate the layout, which seeks to package the information under headings relevant to the essay. Notice that the first heading concerns expectations that slavery would *not* increase. This is relevant to your essay topic, it will help to show why the actual big increase that took place could be considered surprising and needs explanation.

Quotations: none is really needed here, as the author is not citing primary sources or engaging in debate. Conceivably, you might later want to debate whether blacks were inherently suitable, by their nature, for plantation work; Thistlethwaite's phrase 'the best, indeed the only' (labour force) is quoted to identify his view clearly, which you may possibly want to quote if you discuss whether it is correct. Also, you might wish to quote his quite vivid statement about 'the cry for raw cotton', which can be used to make a point succinctly.

Incidentally, this passage offers opportunities to help your essay by *looking up technical or unfamiliar terms*. If you look up 'staple' or 'short-staple', 'lint' and 'gin', you will find out things which might well be worth putting in the essay. A quick internet search will yield some interesting information about Eli Whitney, the American inventor of the cotton gin used for the cotton grown in the South. You might use this information, depending on the amount of detail required by the essay. This shows where the internet can be at its most useful – not so much for debate and interpretation as for straightforward factual information. (But if the information is crucial to your argument, you will need to examine carefully the authority of your source, internet or other.)

Now suppose that the essay question is this: 'In what ways did Britain influence developments in America in the first half of the nineteenth century?' Now your notes will look very different.

	F. Thistlethwaite, *The Great Experiment: An Introduction to the History of the American People,* Cambridge: Cambridge University Press, 1955, pp. 146f.
146	Cases of failure to influence America: ● Slave trade abolished 1807, moves in Britain to abolish slavery (check career of Wilberforce)
147	● But actually slavery grew greatly: ● 1800: about 1m Africans; 1860: 4.5m; these mostly slaves in South Economic influence: ● Demand for cotton: shaped economy of the South – Lancashire's hunger for cotton stimulated cotton production using slave labour ● Crop: 1800: 70,000 bales, 1860: 4 million

Here, there is a section on *failure* to influence because you may want to measure the British influence by looking at ways in which it did and didn't work; you may want to contrast intellectual and ideological influences with hard economic ones. The note '(check career of Wilberforce)' is a reminder for further reading: perhaps you will want to say something about him in the essay and you wish to learn more. (You will quickly find that his dates were 1759–1833, and his object in life was to end slavery.)

Questions

1 Did anything in this chapter strike you as unexpected or surprising? In what ways, if any, do the note-taking methods recommended here differ from your own past practice?

2 From your own experience, what technique or practice would you most recommend to others as a way of taking notes efficiently?

Explanation, Judgment and Historical Imagination

Chapter overview

▶ The past cannot be explained completely.

▶ In past ages, people thought and acted in ways often very different from ours.

▶ Our own culture, with all its customs and standards, is one of an immense historical series; it is not a model by which all the rest should be judged.

▶ Historians have employed various theories about what produces historical change and development; most now seem imperfect.

▶ In studying the past we may find ourselves favouring particular groups in past society, but this has dangers. People's motivations are often shaped by the groups they belong to, but these groups keep changing and are difficult to recognize.

▶ Behaviour also needs to be understood by reference to the standards of the worldview current in a person's civilization.

▶ None of this means that there is no such thing as good or bad, but it can be difficult to recognize good or bad in the context of a past age.

▶ In trying to understand the past we need to cultivate historical imagination – to be able to realize what it was like to live in a different age.

Chapters 1–7 have generally been about the studying that comes before writing an essay. Chapters 9–16 generally concern the writing itself. Here, we are at a point of transition. This chapter is essentially a pause for reflection on the nature of this transition. What happens when you turn from studying to writing?

The limits of historical explanation

Normally your essay is expected to answer a question or solve a problem, *explaining* something by reference to the evidence that has been turned up by your studying. You are to engage in historical explanation. But what is this? How does it differ from biochemical, legal or psychological explanation?

There is no neat answer. The historian, we know, proceeds by looking at what is going on in the context of the phenomena to be explained, and enlarges this context as needed. Things in the context help to explain the phenomena. If you are to make good sense of the context and demonstrate how it can provide, at least, a partial solution to the problem, you need a measure of historical understanding. This is something which comes from profound immersion in the topic and the use of historical imagination. It cannot be pinned down by a scientific formula.

Philosophers have sometimes tried to deal with problems in the philosophy of mind by asking themselves *what it is like* to be a bat, for instance. The historian faces a similar problem in trying to imagine what it was really like to live in past ages, in cultures very different from our own. In a way, the effort of sympathetic imagination is fundamental to the historian's vocation, for only if we can understand *what it was like* to live in past ages can we understand and explain how people behaved.

Yet this goal of explaining the past often looks like chasing the rainbow. It can never be completely achieved because we can never catalogue, assess and analyse *all* the influences on people's behaviour in a particular place or time; to read what they wrote about their motivations can be helpful, but never tells the whole story. People are very rarely aware of all the forces that shape their desires or their perceptions of what is possible.

So history does not seek general laws applicable to the whole of the past and capable of predicting the future reliably. Proof is not the goal. The goal is to achieve the best possible explanation using the best available sources. To demand a perfect explanation is to forbid good ones.[1] Things in the past can be understood better or worse, not completely. We cannot understand even our own lives and times completely.

What this chapter can attempt, however, is to encourage you at least to think about the ways in which various slices of the past were different from our own present. To think about this is to nurture historical imagination. The starting point is to accept that people in some given past age and society did not think about everything in the way that we do, because they lived in a different environment. In medieval France, for example, we should not suppose that what everybody really wanted for their society was democracy as we understand it, if only for the excellent reason that democracy as we understand it was completely unknown to them. It would be unrealistic for us to expect them to think and behave in just the ways that we do, or to suppose that they *ought to*. Their lives were governed by all sorts of conditions which made it impossible for them to apply twenty-first-century standards to their view of the world, or to recognize possibilities of desirable change that we might see. To recognize this truth, and to attempt some understanding of past societies from the little we know about them, is to cultivate historical imagination.

Imagination is not an exact science, and comments on the differences between our own society and those of past ages are bound to be subjective. In the following sections, some suggestions are made about how people have thought about some of these differences, but such suggestions cannot be more than provisional ideas unlikely to apply to all past ages. Do not regard them as hard-edged truths; they are all subject to plenty of debate, and their intended value is simply as a spur to thought about the ways in which things change with changing historical circumstances, and our own experience of the present is not a standard by which to judge everything.

What counts as explanation?

If we decide that something in history, call it X, is explained by something else, Y, it might always be objected that we still have to explain Y. This can lead to an infinite regress. To avoid this, we must be able to accept at some point a particular explanation which fits into a framework of beliefs that satisfies our demand for understanding. What counts as such a framework, and hence as an explanation, depends a great deal on current assumptions and fashions. These change constantly with changing scientific knowledge and cultural outlooks.

Here are some types of explanation of history that have been popular in the past; most of them are likely to leave the historian today less than fully satisfied.

Religion

It has often been supposed that the way people behave can be understood through their religion. Warlike behaviour by a certain community might seem to be explained by their religious beliefs; if they have a warlike religion, that accounts for it.

This sort of explanation, in its most simple form, is outdated; it begs the question. Religions spread among some groups and not others; perhaps warlike religions, if there are such things, spread among warlike people precisely because those people were already warlike and wanted a religion to suit. Again, the characteristics of particular religions and particular groups of people are known to change independently of each other.

Religion in combination with other factors can play a role in historical explanation, however. Max Weber's sociological theory postulates that at certain crucial historical phases, a particular system of religious belief can be decisive, if various other social and economic factors are also present, in determining the course of history.[2]

Race

Darwin's *On The Origin of Species* (published in 1859) profoundly affected thinking about the influence of biological ancestry on human characteristics. It seemed for a while that almost anything might be the result of genetic inheritance – criminality, intelligence, artistic flair, sense of humour, or anything else. In the late nineteenth and early twentieth centuries, such theories seemed to be supported by advanced science, and observation seemed to offer confirmation – particular groups of people with common ancestry behaved in particular ways; therefore, it appeared, their behaviour was the product of heredity.

Nowadays, heredity is not considered to explain many cultural characteristics. The abundant migrations and cultural transformations of the twentieth century demonstrated that social characteristics vary with social and cultural context rather than heredity. People who migrate to places with different cultures are often well assimilated, and their children blend in even better. To attribute group cultural characteristics to racial heredity is to overlook such evidence. Previously, though, the biological explanation of group behaviour appeared to be justified by science.

Overlapping with race as an explanation is *national character* – the notion that citizenship of a particular country could endow one with typical national characteristics, and account for the ways in which countries and their governments behaved. The belief behind this notion was usually that national character was inherited from ancestors. However, it might alternatively be assumed that national character could be absorbed from the environment (even the climate), and could thus be acquired by immigrants.[3]

Economic determinism

The best-known specific theory of economics as the explanation of historical development is that of Karl Marx, who theorized that history must inevitably march through a series of predetermined stages governed by the means and ownership of production – 'primitive communism', slave society, feudalism, capitalism, socialism and communism. At each stage, tensions grow and eventually cause the system to collapse, triggering the next stage. It can be debated how far original Marxism was strictly determinist; some features of it, increasingly exploited by subsequent Marxist thinkers, allowed room for classes or organizations to slow or hasten the succession of historical stages deliberately.

Theories such as this, which fit history to neat patterns, cannot well accommodate the complexity of human experience, and nowadays, for many people, Marxism has lost appeal as a way of accounting for history or predicting the future, but much-modified forms of it have developed. There is now little doubt that economic organization influences social relationships and group behaviour, although the lines of causation are often unclear.

Social classes

Social classes are often defined by economic interests, but there are other definitions. Quite often, history is seen as the product of relationships between classes defined by features of people's parentage, way of life, profession and behaviour in various combinations. These classes, though, exist only to the extent that people in them actually identify themselves by such criteria and, in a crunch, give their loyalty accordingly.

Great men

Historical documents often focus on the doings of individuals. This can encourage the supposition that history is made by the actions of important people – rulers, lords, generals and teachers. Historical changes are brought about by the personality of the most powerful leaders.

On this view, for example, the rise of Nazi Germany might be attributed to the personal qualities and abilities of Adolf Hitler. But for him, the Second World War would not have happened. If a clone of Hitler, with exactly the same personality and attitudes, were raised to adulthood, there would be grave danger of another world war. Today, such notions seem naive. It is nowadays considered that the rise of Nazi Germany came about through some combination of social, economic, cultural and other factors not yet fully understood.

However, the great man theory is helpful in reminding us that history does not obviously follow an iron destiny, and is full of surprises. At various points it can be nudged by chance factors such as the characters of individuals. The actions of a powerful individual, even if not sufficient by themselves to bring about a major historical change, may often be a necessary part of a combination of factors.

Further, study of the role of individuals can be fruitful in advancing our understanding of the past, as in *psychological studies* of historical figures, and *biography* in general.[4]

Conspiracies

Sometimes, historical developments are attributed to conspiracies. Such theories often represent the bias of particular groups with an interest in denying the apparent causes of events or blaming particular opposing groups. Sudden deaths of rulers or powerful statesmen attract conspiracy theories. Particularly familiar is the wealth of speculation about the circumstances surrounding the assassination of President Kennedy. Again, minority racial or religious groups whose wealth or power makes them distrusted by the majority are often targets of conspiracy theories.

Sometimes, though, things really happen as a result of secret plotting, especially when coups, wars or revolutions are launched; unrecorded agreements precede public action, and powerful organizations operating in secret, such as the CIA (which has been blamed in its time for almost everything), may have been responsible for major historical events in ways not generally known.

Institutions

Formal organizations are often powerful groups with a strong hold on their members' loyalties, and to some extent history might be written as the story of relationships between these institutions: monarchies, the Church, guilds or craft associations, the judiciary, armed forces, police forces, secret societies, trade unions, professional bodies (especially in modern society), political parties and many others are institutions which can affect the course of history. Historical explanations often attribute the course of events to the independent behaviour of institutions.

However, the mere existence of an organization with an interest in making events go in a certain way is not, by itself, a full explanation. How did it become powerful enough to influence history? How did it eventually lose this power? From the seventeenth century, the government of the Tokugawa shogunate in Japan created institutions of central control to ensure political stability and keep the outside world at bay. However, by the time a flotilla of American naval vessels commanded by Commodore Perry came in 1853 to demand that it be let in, those institutions of central control had rotted away from within, and the remaining façade quickly crumbled. Why? The rules defining the centralized institutions could not guarantee permanent shogunate control; changes in economics, social relationships or culture eventually robbed them of effectiveness. History cannot be controlled by constructing institutions, for the institutions are themselves subject to the forces of history.

Modern attitudes to historical explanation

Most historians (certainly not all) are reluctant to support uncompromisingly grand theories claiming to explain history as a whole.

Human affairs are enormously complicated and unpredictable, upsetting the predictions of ambitious theories. Generally, historical explanation is directed to particular places and times rather than to the whole canvas of human experience, finding out as much as possible about the immediate context of particular scenes and events and looking for significant influences.

Nevertheless, historians usually favour particular ideas about the sorts of factors that are likely to provide explanations, and favoured ideas follow fashions. Since the later part of the twentieth century, the influences on behaviour of social relationships and economic forces have generally been favoured.

This focus on economic and social factors may eventually be supplanted by other perspectives, and may come to be regarded as a fashion characteristic of a particular period. Every fashion plays its part; theories are tried out, matched against the evidence, and theories that do not work well can be seen for what they are and discarded. (On recent trends in research perspectives, see the Appendix on historiography.)

Should we take sides with favourite groups in history?

In the present state of scientific knowledge, it seems reasonable to suppose that, on the whole, human beings at all times and places have consisted of much the same sort of mixture, with the same inborn range of potential to be good or bad, timid or aggressive, clever or stupid, energetic or lazy. Any substantial random number of people will represent the normal range of human possibilities. What makes a particular group behave well or badly, timidly or aggressively and so on is the influence of the particular place and time in which it finds itself.

This influence may work through culture (beliefs, ideas, values, customs and rituals), economics, social relationships, powerful individuals, or almost anything else in any combination. Perhaps relative wealth produces conditions in which people can reflect on morality and tolerance and learn virtue, or alternatively become lazy and selfish. Perhaps destitution and struggle produce conditions in which people are driven into conflict in order to survive and become callous and evil, or alternatively learn virtue through bitter experience of cruelty and injustice. We cannot pretend to understand completely how it always works.

However, when we study various groups of people in the past, it is natural for all sorts of reasons to identify one as favourite, and then we may find ourselves leaning towards explanations which always justify whatever this group did and said.

We might have various reasons for choosing our favourite group. Perhaps:

- it appears to be a victim of what would be regarded as injustice in today's world
- it consisted of people who appear superficially to be something like us
- it seems to have shared our own political values
- by studying that group we come to see its point of view better than others and start identifying ourselves with it.

These reasons for finding favourites are natural, but not adequate for argument on their behalf – we need first to sort out our real reasons for liking a particular group and try to find good historical evidence for whatever judgments we advance. We must avoid making uncritical judgments without understanding the conditions that influenced people's behaviour.

Did groups exist, or do we invent them?

What constitutes a 'group'? It all depends how people identify themselves; people slide from one way of identifying themselves to another as times change, or in different situations.

We are not entitled to identify a group ('the masses', 'women', 'the Anglo-Saxons', 'the roundheads', 'the creationists', 'the liberals' etc.) and treat them as actors in history until we have *evidence that its members recognized themselves as members of this group and acted to some extent together.* That is, a group that we name is just an invention by us unless we can show that it is *significant.*

However, there are no rules for identifying in advance the significant groups in any given slice of history. The factors that create or dissolve groups can change dramatically. At one point, fierce national loyalty may make a functioning group out of a country's population, but in time new forces may direct loyalties to other group identifications such as religion, sect, language or dialect, or traditional local leaders, and the country may fall apart.

Again, a new law may create group consciousness among those who gain or lose by it; the discovery of a new source of mineral wealth may create group consciousness among those who live in its vicinity and wish to benefit from it. The very identities of groups are transient.

Generally speaking, in modern industrial society people more often identify themselves by broad categories such as the nation, or horizontal strata such as those of occupation, class, education or wealth; in traditional or pre-industrial societies identification is more often by vertical divisions such as family, clan, tribe, or regional groups defined by shared economic activity, dialect, folklore, ritual and myth.

When people identify themselves as members of particular groups with claims on their loyalty, people in one group are distrustful and suspicious about any other group seen to have interests conflicting with their own. When one group has to deal with another, politically, commercially, culturally or in any other way, it expects the worst from the other, and acts accordingly. When one group deals with another that is much less powerful, it tends to exploit it.

The logic of exploitation suggests that groups with conflicting interests must invariably be bitter enemies; but this is not the only rule governing social relations. As anthropologists well know, a group in society with shared interests and reasons to act together is rarely separated from the other groups around it in all possible ways. There are *cross-cutting loyalties* which moderate the suspicion and hostility. We can easily imagine how in some place crop farmers and pastoralists may be two communities with different interests; but any given farming family may recognize bonds of affiliation with any given pastoralist family by shared church attendance, marriage connections, school attended, or favourite hobbies and recreations, so that group identification is somewhat blurred and dissipated. On particular occasions, one loyalty may be dramatically strengthened; on others, it may be diluted.

Further, behaviour is moulded, not only by group allegiance, but also by the principles of the civilization within which a group belongs. This civilization offers a worldview and a set of principles that define the individual's sense of identity. The principles that go with the worldview are strong influences on the range of behaviour people regard as appropriate.

Some historians have tried to map the laws of history by identifying and comparing the civilizations that have arisen over the ages. A famous early example is Arnold Toynbee's work *A Study of History*, published in twelve volumes from 1934 to 1961; he divided the historical record into 26 civilizations, in each of which he detected a similar pattern of religious and other influences. His work displayed immense erudition but is not much cited nowadays. Another theory of civilizations in history was produced by Karl Jaspers (1883–1969), who identified the period roughly 800–200 BC as an 'Axial Age', in which the cultural foundations for all subsequent distinct civilizations were created.

A problem with such theories is that a 'civilization' is not ultimately a hard-edged real thing existing independently of people and groups; it is more like an idea. There is no agreement about the definition or boundaries of a civilization. Civilizations split apart or merge together; they collide with each other and often mingle, even (with sometimes psychologically upsetting results) within the minds of individuals.

Here, we are dealing only in broad generalizations, but these are enough to bring out the complexity of historical reality. We cannot assume that by naming a large collectivity such as a civilization or a small one such as a family we have identified a real solid entity that acted purposefully and predictably in history. To name a group is not to know that it always behaved as one, whether it be 'the Sunni Muslims', 'the French colonizers', 'the middle classes', 'the Church', 'the indigenous people', 'the elite', or 'the masses'. Any one of these names may, at a particular place and time, denote a cohesive functioning group, or it may not.

So we must always use our terminology for human groups cautiously and critically, never supposing that people who can be described in the same way must have behaved in the same way. Society is not a machine; it is more like an organism, or indeed a teeming swarm of organisms, never easily predictable. To have any hope of understanding a past society, learning what life was really like and what factors made people feel that they belonged together, we need to become as familiar as possible with the whole environment of the times.

What things made people in the past different from us?

Obviously, then, we cannot afford to treat the societies of the past as if they were exactly like our own. The study of history should, gradually and cumulatively, develop in us a sense of some of the differences between us and people in the past. The modern age, compared with most past ages, is, in fact, unusual and highly distinctive; since the Industrial Revolution there have been enormous changes in transport, communications, education, law and many other things, producing great changes in people's thinking and behaviour.

Some generalizations about these differences are offered below. They are not to be taken as facts to learn; they are ideas about the general character of the past which might help you to be on your guard against anachronistic interpretations. The broad generalizations that follow cannot be completely true in every case, but they can sensitize you to some of the reasons why people behaved differently:

- *The opinion of 'the masses'*: The masses always existed, and by modern standards they were usually suffering, but they did not usually recognize themselves as 'the masses' of the citizenry in our sense, or even (if they knew no other situation) as suffering. People travelled much less; not many were literate and few read newspapers, even if newspapers existed; people were divided by language and dialect, religious allegiance, market orientations. Most loyalties were local – to the clan, the village, the patron whose protection was needed. Therefore, it might be unwise to make assumptions about what 'the masses' wanted on the analogy of the way things are in our own society.

- *Corruption*: Political life was vastly more insecure than in modern industrialized countries; government tended to be arbitrary, unpredictable and subject to violent change; positions in government service were obtained by personal connections rather than professional advance. Civil service pay was often minimal. Political and official life was regulated chiefly by deals between individuals and factions. Such behaviour could be necessary to their survival. What would be called 'corruption' in our society was often simply the normal and natural form of behaviour for people with insecure and temporary authority.

- *Welfare*: All countries were much poorer than modern industrialized nations, and constantly preoccupied with war or the threat of war on their frontiers. Governments could not afford to concern themselves with much more than law and order. They often lacked centralized revenue systems and had to bargain with local elites for revenue. There was no room for the modern assumption that a government must provide regularly and predictably for the welfare of the disadvantaged.

- *Women's lot*: Most people lived, by our standards, in dire poverty. Infant mortality was extremely high. Lives were shorter than those of people in modern societies. Care of the old devolved to their children. Therefore, most women spent much of their adult lives giving birth to and looking after a succession of babies. There were no modern facilities to lighten housework and childcare, yet most of the breadwinning work outside the home was even more gruelling than housework. Most women found it natural to devote themselves to the home, and, however intelligent, they did not become a body of opinion on matters of public concern. Today, we do not judge this situation as desirable; but there was little alternative then.

- *Violence*: Political conflicts were violent, and the fate of losers was usually harsh. Punishment of crime was harsh. Life was harsh. The peace and relative stability which we take for granted as a natural state of affairs had to be struggled for. In this world, all parties exploited others when they could. Conditions then were much closer to the 'state of nature' described by Hobbes in *Leviathan,* in which life was 'poor, nasty, brutish and short'.

In a poor society without technological advances, life had to be very different from what is taken for granted in our own society. It should not be surprising to find that, by our standards, people often behaved in ways that were bigoted, racist, corrupt, undemocratic, or cruel. When we learn of such behaviour in a particular case, we need to realize that it may have been typical of the age, and should not be treated as if it were exceptional.

So when you look for the answer to a historical question, you need to consider carefully what sort of assumptions can be made about people's behaviour, and avoid anachronistic judgments.

Historical imagination

Successful historical study is not a matter of reading hard facts from a database. It is a matter of immersing ourselves as deeply as possible in other people's worlds, so that we may develop a sense of why they felt as they did, why they liked things we do not like, and never thought of things that seem obvious to us. It may come as a shock when we read that people who at first seemed decent had views totally unlike ours on subjects such as capital punishment, the treatment of animals or disabled people, democracy, human rights, arranged marriages, or the status of women. Such shocks do not mean that these people were after all less deserving of our sympathy; in most cases, study will show that these views were natural ones to take in the cultural environments in which people lived. Sometimes, further study may suggest that some of these alien-looking attitudes were not unreasonable, given the circumstances. We must approach an unfamiliar world with an open mind.

To withhold sympathy from past ages on principle, treating it as a blight or defect not to have the benefit of our civilization and our values, would show a lack of historical imagination. In future ages, things will have changed again, and people may look back on us with disdain, incredulous and horrified that we eat meat, send old people to retirement homes, put criminals in prison, drive cars, keep pets, waste water, pay income tax, or join the army; there is no telling what attitudes and customs will in the future be thrown into the dustbin. If we could confront the accusations of future ages, we would be anxious to explain that our customs are natural in our circumstances. We should likewise seek to understand why people in the past found their usages natural.

Questions

1 The Tokugawa shogunate is mentioned above as an example of an institution that rotted from within. Considering periods and places in history that you have studied, identify another particular group, class or organization that became powerful and drew on the strong loyalty of its members for a while, before ultimately losing power; what are the most likely historical reasons for its rise and fall?

2 Adding a further item to the list in the section 'What things made people in the past different from us?', identify and discuss one respect in which life in pre-industrial societies in general was basically different from our own, in ways that affected people's experiences, assumptions and values.

3 Should historians be bolder in the quest for a theory explaining the pattern of world history, following in the footsteps of Toynbee and Jaspers?

4 Blaise Pascal (1623–62), a hugely versatile philosopher and mathematician, claimed that if Cleopatra's nose had been of a different shape, the course of history would have run quite differently. Find out what you can in a few minutes about the meaning and implications of Pascal's idea. Is it important to the understanding of history, or may it be misleading?

Chapter

9

Planning

Chapter overview

- ► An essay is a piece of engineering requiring a question, an approach, evidence, reasoning and conclusion.
- ► Everything about an essay needs to be geared to the title, which expresses the question set.
- ► The introduction must clarify the title if any clarification is needed.
- ► Most essays are designed to require exploration of some problem of debate and conflicting evidence, which you need to recognize and confront.
- ► Your essay should have a clear plan of attack, indicating, for example, whether its structure will be narrative, thematic or historiographical.
- ► The evidence adduced should be just what is needed to carry the weight of your argument, and not more.
- ► The reasoning supporting the conclusion must be adequate, demonstrating appropriate correlations, testimony, etc.

An essay expresses what the writer thinks about a certain topic. It must show plainly what the topic is and what the writer thinks. How do you set about planning your essay so as to achieve these goals?

Deciding on essentials

Planning involves identifying a question and an answer and joining them together with evidence and reasoning. It does not involve assembling a mass of material and then cutting out less important-seeming parts to reach the right length.

Start with the simplest possible statement of what you think. This statement alone will determine what material is relevant. Do not proceed to construct the essay before you can put the essential argument in a nutshell.

What comes after that? Students sometimes ask: 'How much of it should consist of ... (facts, ideas, background, introduction, narrative, evidence, and so on)?' But a good essay cannot be achieved by making sure that two-thirds of it consists of facts and one-third of ideas, or by writing an introduction 350 words long, or by supporting the conclusion with three different arguments.

The answer cannot be given by stating a quantity, because it is not the quantity of anything in the essay that makes it good. What makes essay content good is *appropriateness to the argument*. The interpretation of concepts, introduction, background, or any other ingredient is sufficient when it succeeds in supplying what the argument needs, not when it reaches a certain length.

Here, 'argument' means the clear demonstration, by the evidence found in the best available range of sources cited, that your answer to the given question is the best available. This demonstration grows organically from the question. All the parts of it belong together.

The cycle of argument

Here is a summary of the ingredients in the cycle of argument (see Chapter 3, '... and proceeds to an answer', pp. 23–4), as related to the planning process:

1 **The question itself**
   Identify the question. The question grows directly from the title, which is therefore one of the most important parts of your essay; your essay will be judged by its success in answering the question. Think carefully about its exact meaning.
2 **An introduction**
   Make clear what approach you are going to adopt. There may be different possible interpretations of the question; and there may be different ways of organizing your material, such as narrative, thematic or historiographical.
   Set out necessary background information. But do not go beyond background material that is necessary to explain things you will say in your discussion.
3 **The factual evidence you need**
   Show the *evidence*, citing sources in which you have found it. Your factual evidence will be the most relevant and significant available to test possible answers to the central question.
4 **Critical assessment of the evidence**
   Show exactly how and why the evidence you have mentioned has compelled you to come to certain conclusions.

5 **Your conclusions**

Offer conclusions related to the original question. Remember that the argument that earns points for a good essay is not the argument that is in your mind; it is the argument that is completely clear and logically articulated in the essay.

The introduction

The introduction to your essay is in one way the most important part. Everything that follows must grow out of it, so if you do not get the beginnings right the whole essay will be disabled.

In the cycle of argument discussed above, elements 1 and 2 belong to the introduction. This does not mean that the introduction should occupy two-fifths of the essay; a single paragraph may be sufficient. Nor does it mean that some minimum number of words must be addressed to each of these elements in order to deal with them. What goes into the introduction depends entirely on what is necessary to show what the problem is, how the question is to be interpreted, and how you plan to answer it. Some elements may not require any immediate discussion; for example, the meaning of the words in the title may be perfectly obvious, or there may be no need to spend any time sketching in background.

Defining terms in the title

Suppose that you are answering the question: 'How far was the Meiji Restoration influenced by indigenous Japanese ways of thinking?' To make clear how you understand this question, you might wish to say something about the meaning of 'indigenous', and you will certainly need to say what the Meiji Restoration was, but it is most unlikely that anything will be gained by looking up and reporting the dictionary meaning of 'influenced' or 'thinking'. A discussion of the meaning of a term is justified only to the extent that *it has a bearing on your later discussion*. Giving definitions has no virtue in its own right.

There is no point in defining a term unless you know what you are going to do with the definition later; it affects the way you answer the question. Take the question about the Meiji Restoration. Suppose you wish to argue that, in certain ways, Buddhist ideas played a part in the movement. Now, Buddhism did not originate in Japan; it came directly from China and Korea, ultimately from India. So it was not strictly indigenous. But, on the other hand, it had made itself an integral part of Japanese culture for over a thousand years. Does it count as indigenous or not for the purpose of the question?

Using a dictionary may or may not be the right way to go about it; perhaps your common sense will suggest that what matters is the thought behind the question, which is an invitation to distinguish modern western influences on the Meiji Restoration from traditional ones within Japan. In any event, something will need to be said about the meaning of 'indigenous' *if you want to talk about Buddhism*. If you do not, there may be no point in worrying at all about the exact meaning of the word 'indigenous'. This is one more case where it is necessary to recognize that what you put in the essay must be directly related to the argument.

What makes a question historically interesting?

The real *point* of an essay question is often about some problem of understanding that has intensely interested historians; if so, you need to understand thoroughly why, and what are the contrasting points of view driving the historians whose work you read. What agenda lie behind their arguments? What do they really want to prove?

Take, as an example, the question whether the living standard of British industrial workers was rising or falling in the first half of the nineteenth century. It was a famous controversy, with two historians, Hartwell and Hobsbawm, as leading protagonists. Without any background knowledge, you might think that the question is a fairly dry matter of detail – the Industrial Revolution took either a shorter time or a longer time to bring about an improvement in ordinary workers' standards of living, and a cool assessment of the evidence ought to settle the matter.

However, large issues of fierce debate lurk in the background. Some people think that the Industrial Revolution was driven by a selfish doctrine of profit, that the early industrialists did not care for the welfare of their employees, and that industrialization caused avoidable misery to the workers for a long time. Economic forces, they say, cannot be left to themselves; in the interests of the poor and vulnerable, government should intervene. Other people think that government management is often harmful to the operation of the economy, and that the role of capitalists in the Industrial Revolution was fundamentally benign.

To some extent, the question about living standards acts as a proxy for these two opposed philosophical points of view. As you read, your recognition of the underlying points of view of different historians will help you see the point of their arguments.

Explaining your approach

If there are different ways of taking the question, the approach you adopt may reflect any of the following sorts of choices:

1 You may choose one *interpretation* of the question itself in preference to others.

2 You may choose to give attention to some particular *aspects* of the question, or some particular sub-questions, because they seem most fruitful.

3 You may choose one principle rather than another to govern the sequence of topics or events which you discuss. (This question is taken up in the next section.)

Whatever choices you make, ensure that the introduction includes whatever explanation of your procedures will help the reader see what you are doing. Your reader is not sitting inside your head watching your thoughts, and cannot be expected to see the point of everything you say unless you explain how it all fits together.

The plan of attack

Next, choose the sequence of topics or events to be discussed. Various approaches are possible, and only you can decide which is right for your particular essay. Every approach has its own advantages and its own dangers. Here are three major types of approach, with comments on the pros and cons of each; consider these in order to decide which is right for your purpose.

The narrative approach

You may deal with the material by going through it chronologically, telling a story and commenting as often as needed on what the material shows in relation to the question.

Advantages

Sometimes, this approach is dismissed as 'mere narrative', as if there were something wrong with telling a story (although narrative has been enjoying a revival). This is quite false. What matters is *how* the story is told. So long as the significance of each episode for the essay's central argument is clearly brought out, a narrative approach can succeed better than any other. It can make vivid the situations in which people found themselves, and thereby account for their actions.

Take the question: 'Why did the Dutch ultimately fail to re-establish their empire in the East Indies after the Japanese occupation?' A narrative approach might suit your purpose well if you think that the failure is best understood by looking at a number of weaknesses in the Dutch position that were brought out successively as the struggle to re-establish the empire proceeded. You will then tell the story of this struggle, selecting for attention those events that help to illustrate the weaknesses in the Dutch position. At each point, you will show how the Dutch were prevented from achieving certain goals because of the concrete situation in which they found themselves: their behaviour can be seen in its proper context. Whether this approach is actually the best one, though, must depend on its appropriateness to your answer to the question.

Disadvantages

The danger of the narrative approach is that, in telling a story, you may quickly become bogged down in the detail and lose sight of the conclusions which are supposed to give meaning to the whole essay. A teacher may complain that there is too much narrative, or that the essay suffers from being in a narrative form. This would mean that, in this particular essay, the shape of the wood has become obscured by all the trees – the reasoning leading to the answer to the question is concealed by the step-by-step progress of the narrative. It is particularly important in a narrative treatment to make plain the connection of every stage of the story to the underlying argument.

The thematic approach

You may deal with the material by treating successively a number of themes or aspects of the topic, and discussing the evidence that is relevant to each in turn.

Advantages

In a way, the thematic approach is the safest one, because, by its nature, it shows that you are tackling the problem analytically, and the particular themes that are identified give a clear outline of your analytical scheme. Take the question about the Dutch in Indonesia considered above. Possibly you will decide that the answer is not to be found in the successive episodes of the struggle to reimpose Dutch authority. You may prefer to look elsewhere, to such factors as:

- the political and economic situation in Holland after the Second World War
- American policy and American pressures exercised on the Dutch government
- the experience of young Javanese people during Japanese occupation
- the infection of nationalism from other parts of Asia.

You may then do best to discuss each of these in turn, showing how important each is.

Disadvantages

Using the thematic method, you can identify a number of possibly important subtopics or themes; but how do you decide which of them are more important than others? This can be difficult, and may require deeper digging into the detail of the episodes that drove people to act as they did.

Too much concentration on amassing a list of relevant themes may risk squeezing out the all-important exercise of independent thought that enables you to make your own judgment of the most important themes.

The historiographical approach

You may deal with the material by examining a number of possible answers to the question set, discussing the evidence that is relevant to each of these in turn and referring to the arguments of historians who have favoured each answer.

Advantages

The historiographical approach, by its nature, keeps your discussion on the track required by the question: all the material is arranged according to different possible answers. It may be particularly appropriate when the question refers to a specific controversy, with particular historians arguing for conflicting points of view.

In following this approach you must identify the arguments in turn; you need to group together historians who are essentially offering the same answer, but show carefully whatever significant differences there may be between them alongside the shared conclusions.

Sometimes, you will have to decide how to treat historians who do not specifically discuss the question with which you are concerned but who provide relevant facts and ideas. Show how their material can be fitted into the logic of the debate you are analysing. Your astuteness in identifying and classifying the possible arguments, comparing them with each other and pointing to ways in which evidence actually supports or fails to support particular conclusions, will help to make your essay something more than a mere report of what different historians have said.

Disadvantages

A trap with the historiographical approach is that you may be tempted to rest content with a mere summary of one point of view after another, without making any independent comments. Such essays may not rise above the level of such a report – they do no more than record the arguments of others – and at the end of them there is often no conclusion reflecting independent thought. It is particularly important to be able to offer thoughtful reflective comments on the historians you discuss. You are not required to prove that one side in a debate is wrong and the other right, but you do need to show the quality of your own thought in the way you summarize, analyse and compare; wherever it is possible, comment on the quality of the evidence and reasoning deployed by your authorities.

Whatever the order in which you arrange the points of view you discuss, there must be a reason for it. Perhaps you will start with the views that are most easily criticized and end with the case that seems strongest. Do not simply summarize the different points of view without comparing their strengths and weaknesses. Make sure that you have something of your own to put in.

Choosing the evidence to put in

Throughout most sections of your essay, you will introduce evidence, with footnotes, to support what you say. What counts as evidence? Deciding what evidence to put in requires, in the first place, that you should be able to recognize those facts that you have read in your sources which deserve to be treated as evidence, and not as opinions which could be debated. This was discussed in Chapter 6 ('Distinguishing between factual evidence and judgment or opinion', pp. 53–5).

Evidence consists of propositions that can be considered true ('William arrived early in the morning'; 'On average factory workers earned slightly more in 1840 than in 1830'). Such a statement can be used as evidence *providing that there is no reason for distrusting it. If you can see any reason why it might be wrong, or why other writers might want to dispute it, do not treat it as a fact.*

But what particular pieces of evidence deserve to be cited in the essay? Faced with a mass of notes, students often wonder how to select the particular facts (statements that can be treated as factual evidence) that go in. Selection should be governed by:

- *The question at issue*: When this is properly defined, it should be easy to see what is relevant to it and what is not.

- *Your chosen approach to it*: When you have set out the way in which you are going to tackle the issue, this should show what needs to be looked at particularly.

- *Your argument*: When you have completed your reading and thought about it, you can decide what your answer to the question will be. Be your own devil's advocate, challenging yourself to justify the answer you are giving. If you cannot justify what you want to say, then change it. Ask yourself: *what is it that really convinces me that this is the best solution to the problem?* When you have given yourself the answer to that question, you will be able to recognize what pieces of evidence are necessary to support what you want to say.

- *The best possible counter-argument*: You need to take full account, not only of what supports your argument, but also of the best case that could be made against it. Your essay should attend to this counter-argument and, as far as possible, dispose of it.

An example

Suppose that the question set is 'Why did the number of slaves in America increase in the first half of the nineteenth century?' Referring to the sample note layout in Chapter 7 (pp. 66–8), you will see that the paragraph quoted there from a book contains some relevant material. If we confine ourselves, for simplicity, to this material, it becomes easy to see how some useful evidence can be identified. A highly condensed version of what you might say in your essay is as follows:

> So there was a big increase in the number of slaves in the South during the period, and it coincided with the widespread adoption of cotton as the staple of production. This is not a coincidence. Several factors encouraged cotton growers to use slave labour on their fields. To begin with, there was already a tradition of slave labour in the area, in the production of various other previously favoured crops; indeed, according to Thistlethwaite, slaves were the 'best, indeed the only' suitable and available labour force.[1] Members of slave families were usually accustomed to working in the tough, hot conditions of the cotton fields;[2] their culture did not encourage them in any expectation of vastly better working conditions.[3] Further, the economics of the situation were decisive: the slaves were cheap to use, satisfied with plain food and accustomed to no more than basic housing and clothing.[4]

However, this paragraph represents an oversimplification of what an essay should be. In the example, all four notes would refer to a single page in a general survey of American history. A good essay would have to exploit a reasonable range of sources, and even if the basic factual information represented by this paragraph came originally from one book, you would expect by the time you wrote the essay to be able to fill out this material and enrich it with a great deal of detail from other sources. The paragraph above would then turn into a series of sections on aspects of the slave labour force, perhaps occupying several pages at the heart of the essay, and with footnotes citing various sources. The paragraph nevertheless serves to show how facts used in evidence are presented to support a claim you are making.

The logic of your argument

Remember that history is an art in some ways and a craft in other ways. A historical argument requires imagination, but it also requires engineering. Your essay must be engineered, precisely articulating question, approach, evidence, reasoning and conclusion. Like the stones which form a true arch, these five elements must be a good tight fit. Consider, as you plan, what material is essential and what is not. Knowing what to exclude is a hallmark of competence in essay construction.

Evidence is linked to conclusions by reasoning. Make sure that the steps in the reasoning are made quite explicit in the essay. This 'reasoning' component of an essay is, of course, not a separate section that you write after all the evidence has been recorded and before the conclusion. It is embodied throughout in all the comments you make on the significance of the evidence and in the links between successive sections.

How an argument is built: an example

Here is an example. Suppose that you have been asked to account for the persecution of Christianity in the Roman Empire, a question that is worth asking since, superficially at least, Rome seems to have been very tolerant of different religions.

The answer is certainly not straightforward, and there are various factors which ought to be considered. Perhaps you feel that people must have turned against Christianity because of political and economic insecurity and instability, and you succeed in collecting together various pieces of evidence of impoverishment, displacement, riots and so on during the period when the persecutions took place. Do you have the makings of an argument?

Probably not, unless more conditions are fulfilled. If you look, you can find examples of insecurity and instability everywhere at any time. Nothing is explained by showing that they existed in the Roman Empire. You must show that there is something particularly significant about the problems of this particular period; evidence must be found that they are distinctly more acute than in earlier times or in other places. Even then, nothing is proved. Beware of arguing, in effect, that when situation X is present and event Y occurs, X must be the cause of Y. For example, by 1928, women in Britain aged over 21 could vote. A few years later, Europe was engulfed by economic depression, war, genocide, massive destruction and displacement of populations. Few suggest that all such horrors were a direct result of giving women the vote.

In order to make a respectable case for a link between sociopolitical insecurity and persecution of Christianity, you need to find some good evidence of a real causal link. This could be:

- evidence that the particular territories where persecution was most virulent happened to be precisely those with the worst social problems
- evidence that territories without problems also lacked persecutions
- an official report recommending a bout of persecution as a way to distract people from grievances which might promote sedition.

The third sort is the most direct. Preferably, you should find all three of these. Generally speaking, when you want to argue that Y happened because of X, you need to be able to show that wherever X was present, Y occurred (or, if it did not, one can see the particular reason why), that whenever Y occurred X was present (or, if it did not, why the situation was in some way exceptional), and that the steps by which X gave rise to Y can, in some cases, be seen in detail.

The conclusion

In the planning stage, it is certainly desirable to think about what you will say in the conclusion. The whole essay leads up to it; it defines your answer to the question. Throughout the construction of the essay, keep in mind how each detail of the composition contributes to the argument supporting your conclusion.

However, in real life, it is remarkable how things change as you go along. It will probably turn out that only as you write out the essay can you finally understand what exactly you are saying. Only when you come to write the conclusion will you see just what is needed to add the right finishing touch. Therefore, more specific comments on this process are offered in Chapter 11, 'Writing the conclusion' (pp. 109–10).

Questions

1 After a quick Internet search to find out what sort of book is Francis Fukuyama's *The End of History and the Last Man*, say what elements you would wish to include in the introductory section of an essay titled 'Was Fukuyama right about the "End of History"?'

2 Suggest ways of turning the following essay topics into questions that raise potentially interesting problems, without significantly changing the subject: 'The American Civil War'; 'The rise of Hitler'; 'The fall of Rome'; 'The Spanish Armada'; 'The European discovery of Australia'.

3 After a brief consultation of reference sources to find out a little about the subject, consider how you might go about writing an essay under the title 'The Glorious Revolution of 1688: treason, restoration or pragmatism?' Are there words in the title the definition of which you would wish to discuss in the introduction of your essay? Explain why, or why not.

10

Writing and Independent Thought

Chapter overview

▶ Your essay is essentially a statement of what you think about something, and not what somebody else thinks.

▶ If you read a book questioningly, looking for points of doubt or debate, you will probably have thoughts about it, and these thoughts are just what is wanted to make an essay grow.

▶ Making succinct notes on something gives you practice in making summaries.

▶ Summarizing books or articles succinctly is a good way to kick-start your independent thoughts about them.

▶ There are various ways in which your essay writing can show your independent thought.

▶ Plagiarism is writing in such a way that it appears that what you say is your own thought, when it isn't.

▶ Paraphrasing is plagiarism if it is used to express somebody else's idea, interpretation or judgment without proper acknowledgement.

▶ Paraphrasing is not plagiarism if it is used simply to report straightforward factual information.

Deciding what to write can be difficult. The problem may be expressed in words like these: 'The authors of the books I have read know vastly more than I do. I cannot improve on what they say, and I would feel ridiculous trying. How can I say anything new and independent?'

This feeling is natural, but it misses the point. What is an essay supposed to be? The job of academic authors is to say what they think about historical problems after looking at the *best sources available anywhere*. Your job in a student essay is to say what you think after looking at the *best sources available to you within a particular period*. You are not supposed to express thoughts about the historical problems that are as good as the thoughts in the books. You are expected only to express the sorts of thoughts which can reasonably be expected after doing just the reading that you can do.

How independent thought is applied

Suppose that you are to write an essay about Machiavelli ('How do you account for Machiavelli's ideas about how a ruler should treat enemies?'), and you have read books in which the imaginary paragraphs offered in Chapter 1 (pp. 4–5) occur. After doing the reading, some thoughts may occur to you. For example, if pressed, you might say something like:

> Well, this first book seems to say that neighbouring countries are always likely to go to war with each other, but that's not always true, is it? Sometimes countries can get along all right with each other. This fourth book seems to say something like that. It suggests that if the really big countries in the area had been afraid to fight each other, they might have used their influence to stop the little countries fighting each other too so as to avoid being dragged into a big war, like the Cold War I suppose, and then there would have been only very limited wars, border fighting perhaps, things like that. Then Machiavelli would have looked around at the way things worked in his world and seen them differently. He might not have said that rulers always ought to be cruel and treacherous, because in a safer region that sort of behaviour might not be necessary.

This is a perfectly reasonable thought. Not all thoughts will be relevant to the essay, but those that are can be developed into a discussion of the things you have read, explaining what you think. With only a little tweaking, the passage above could be worked up into a part of the essay:

So we see that Machiavelli did not hesitate to preach cruel and treacherous behaviour on the part of the ruler. There are different ways of understanding why he should have done so.

One view, the realist theory, is that because there is no world government it is impossible for neighbouring states to regulate their dealings with each other peacefully, and conflict is inevitable. Survival requires extreme measures; the ruler cannot afford to follow the principles of a categorical moral code.[1] Machiavelli's experience had taught him to be a realist. Therefore he recommended extreme measures. This view is represented by J. Smith.[2]

Some modification of this interpretation may be necessary: Machiavelli may have been influenced by conditions affecting his own place and time rather that

(Continued)

universal ones. Perhaps it is significant that northern Italy in his time was subjected to constant turmoil by the invasions of competing larger powers, which made impossible any system of sustained peaceful coexistence. Machiavelli's ideas can in this sense, as T. Brown argues, be seen as a product of his own environment.[3]

[1] As described by S. Robinson, *Machiavelli and Moral Philosophy*, London 2000, p. 100.
[2] J. Smith, *Machiavelli and Political Science*, New York 2001, p. 101.
[3] T. Brown, *Machiavelli and History*, Melbourne 2002, p. 102.

There is nothing strikingly insightful in this passage, but, taken in conjunction with the imaginary source material used, it shows how one's own natural independent response to the reading might prompt a thoughtful section of argument in an essay. Notice that the imaginary student here refrains from quoting slabs from the books; he thinks that the points can be adequately and succinctly made in his own words, but he uses footnotes as well as acknowledgements in the text to indicate that he is depending in certain ways on particular passages in books, which are fully cited, with page references to aid verification.

So what is wanted in an essay is independent thought *about* what you have read, not a *repetition* of what you have read. It is the independent thought that makes the essay good or bad. You do not have to display it by saying better things than the books say; you can display it by offering your own reflection on what you have read. It shows in various ways:

- *The ability to identify significant passages and recognize how they are relevant to your purposes.* In the example above, independent thought is shown simply by identifying the significant remarks by 'J. Smith' and 'T. Brown' and showing how they are relevant.

- *The ability to summarize accurately and succinctly what is said about relevant points in your sources.* For example, the last paragraph in the example above summarizes what is relevant in the book by 'T. Brown'. The ability to put just what is relevant succinctly into your own words shows your understanding of what you have read and its relevance.

- *The ability to make connections between what is said in two different sources.* 'S. Robinson's' distinction between different systems of ethical judgment is related to the description of Machiavelli's ideas about the ruler's behaviour.

- *The ability to detect inconsistencies between what is said in two or more books.* There could be an inconsistency between 'J. Smith' and

'T. Brown', the first suggesting that unprincipled and treacherous international relations are universal, the second that they characterize a particular environment such as that of northern Italy in Machiavelli's time. You could point this out in your essay, but it would be important to make sure by closer reading and quotation that the disagreement is real.

- *The ability to find evidence in one place for what is said in another.* It would be good, for example, to find passages in Machiavelli's *The Prince* which support what is said by 'Smith' or 'Brown', and if they are distinctly relevant to your argument they could usefully be quoted in support. This would show that you are using your own thought.

- *The ability to find weaknesses in the argument of some authority.* Your essay might possibly benefit from criticizing 'J. Smith' more explicitly, arguing that the system of international relations portrayed by Machiavelli is not universal but characterizes some places and periods more than others. (You would need to make the criticism carefully, being fully fair to 'Smith'.)

Thus, there are various ways in which, without being qualified to carry out original research, a student can display independent thought in an essay by exploiting and reflecting on the sources. These are the things that earn points, not the assembling and repetition of information. It is fundamental to the nature of an essay that it should display independent thought in such ways, and be written in the writer's own words except for quotations for specific purposes.

Identifying plagiarism

Students sometimes write passages in their essays that are technically plagiarism without intending to do anything wrong; thus, it is important to be aware of what plagiarism is and to avoid it. Plagiarism is often discussed in ways that make it seem mysterious and dangerous. From what you hear or read about plagiarism, you might receive the impression that it is something extremely difficult to recognize, like a bear trap dug specially to catch unwary students and make them feel that further study is hopeless because they will never know when they are doing something wrong.

However, there is no need to feel like this. You can take reassurance from two thoughts:

1 It is true that ideally the experience of studying at school should result in students understanding exactly what essays are supposed to be and

incapable of plagiarizing by accident, but, in fact, as your teacher probably understands perfectly well, there are students who have never been given a proper explanation and have not managed to work out what plagiarism is and what is wrong with it.

2   An essay is an exercise in independent thought, and, once you understand that, it is not particularly difficult to see what is needed and why repeating things in a literal-minded way from books is not the right way to write essays.

The object of this section is to deal with the problem, removing the mystery and danger. Actually, the job is already half done, because everything that has been said here about independent thought forms part of the explanation of plagiarism, even without mentioning the P-word. Independent thought has been analysed on earlier pages as essential to an essay, and plagiarism is just the opposite of independent thought.

Plagiarism is defined as *presenting some piece of work as one's own when in fact the content of the work is somebody else's*. In a rather broad sense, plagiarism is putting somebody else's ideas into what you write in such a way as to make the reader think that they are your ideas. For practical purposes, plagiarism is (in a narrower sense) *copying out* what another has written and giving the impression that what is thus copied is one's own work.

Sometimes, students know that it is wrong to copy out sentences from sources into their essays, so *paraphrase* them instead. But paraphrasing is still plagiarism. Paraphrasing is basically like copying out; it is editing what is copied by changing words here and there, so that it reads differently, and commonly leaving bits out, either to make the result shorter, or because the copyist does not understand some passages and feels safer without them. A paraphrase of what somebody else has said is not an exercise in expressing your own thought; it is plagiarism.

In your essay, all the words must be your own unless you acknowledge that they are being borrowed from a named source and identify them by inverted commas as *quotation*.

Copying out and paraphrasing should be easy enough to avoid. In making notes, it is important not to risk writing out quotations from books you read in such a way that you may later mistake them for your own words and then repeat them in the actual essay; if words not your own appear in the essay, they must be identified as quotations. Unacknowledged quotations are plagiarism (see Chapter 7, 'Do not copy out verbatim from books', pp. 64–5). One rotten apple can send bad a barrel-load. One plagiarised sentence in an essay can make the reader wonder whether the whole essay is plagiarised, and it may be rejected.

Paraphrasing in presenting factual evidence

The remarks above step around a particular problem that actually requires a little more discussion: can you reasonably be expected to avoid paraphrasing when you are simply presenting factual evidence? On occasion, you may find that it is extremely difficult to make some particular point in your essay without using many of the same words as the book from which you derived the material. Any attempt to avoid paraphrasing by expressing yourself in a totally different way may justly seem an artificial and pointless exercise. What happens then?

In order to solve this problem, it is necessary to remember the distinction between an *idea, judgment* or *interpretation* – that is, a piece of thought by the writer of your source – and a point which reports what seems to be a fact – that is, a piece of *evidence*. (See Chapter 6, 'Distinguishing between factual evidence and judgment or opinion', pp. 53–5.) Once this distinction is clear, the solution becomes easy.

Let us reconsider the two things in turn. If you find yourself paraphrasing an *idea* or *opinion* of the author of something you have read, you are thereby giving the impression that somebody else's thought is your own. Suppose that you read the following passage in a book:

> The city workers did not go into revolt, but their rallies and near-riots had the effect of changing the rules of the political game – no longer could people sustain the old notion that the wealthy oligarchs had a divine right to rule.

Suppose that you write the following passage in your essay:

> The urban poor did not stage a rebellion, but their demonstrations and noisy protests effectively changed the old rules by which people believed the rich ruling class governed by divine right.

In this case, the original is being paraphrased. It certainly gives a false impression. The author of the original has an idea to express – he wants to distinguish between outright armed revolt and a much lesser degree of unrest, marked by a certain amount of commotion, and he wants to argue that even this lesser degree of unrest was enough to change the way people thought about the political order in which they lived. That is, he refers to some facts and presents his idea about their significance. He is thus presenting an argument or idea of his own. But if you paraphrase it without saying that the idea is the original author's, you are, in effect, pretending that it is your own idea. That is different from summing it up in your own words and saying that it is his idea (which is what you should do). The false impression given is that somebody else's idea is yours. To avoid this, write something like:

> Smith claims that, though this civil unrest did not amount to rebellion, it was severe enough to put an end to the old unthinking assumption that the rich had a 'divine right' to power.[1]

Here, an idea is presented in a way that does not give the false impression that it is your own.

But now suppose that you want to use, not an idea, but a statement of fact that can be used as *evidence* in your argument. The original source says this:

> The city workers staged a number of noisy rallies that went out of control.

Here, you may wish to use this fact, and you will report it in your essay, with a footnote so that the reader can verify your source for the fact. How will you describe the fact? You may try various ways of saying that the urban workers took part in various demonstrations that had a way of ending in violence, but if they are accurate statements of what your source told you, they will all look like paraphrases of the original:

> Various rather violent demonstrations were put on by the urban workers, and these became uncontrollable.[1]

> The workers in the town were responsible for some turbulent protest rallies which became violent.[1]

However you put it, it looks like a paraphrase of the original. But no harm is being done; you are merely reporting what you have found out, and your footnote will adequately signal to the reader what you are doing. You are not repeating somebody's idea as if it were you are own; you are using somebody as the authority for a statement of fact, which is documented with a footnote. The statement of fact will then take its place in your argument, which truly expresses your own ideas.

This is an important case in which it is necessary to be able to distinguish between identifying something you have read as *factual evidence* and identifying it as an *idea, opinion, judgment or interpretation*, something that might be argued about. The ability to signal this distinction is a good mark of an essay writer's historical sensitivity.

Good and bad use of what you read: a longer example

Now we can take a more substantial case to illustrate the use of independent thought. First read the following paragraph. It is from C.P. Fitzgerald, *China: A Short Cultural History*, London 1961, p. 88. Then look at the paragraphs A and B that follow. Each is an imaginary extract from an imaginary student

essay written to the question: 'What are the essentials of Confucianism?'
One paragraph represents the proper use of source material in essay
writing; the other represents a paraphrase, without any real independent
thought.

At first reading, both paragraphs might seem all right, but it is worth
persevering with the exercise and discovering the differences between the
two passages by studying the notes following them. (For ease of
comparison, the sentences in the original paragraph by Fitzgerald are
prefaced by numbers; the sentences in the sample essay paragraphs bear
numbers approximately corresponding to the parts of the original on
which they are based.)

> [1] It is difficult to escape the feeling that Confucian doctrine is based on a
> shrewd appreciation of the real character of the Chinese people, and
> endeavours to stimulate by precept and regulation the qualities which are not
> naturally well developed in the national character. [2] Like the reformers of the
> modern age, Confucius deplored the particularism of his countrymen, and
> emphasised the virtues of filial submission and loyalty, virtues which, as he
> himself attests, were all too rare among his contemporaries. [3] The Confucian
> insistence on filial duty and the strict training of the young would seem harsh
> until it is realized that the Chinese, a people naturally over-kind and indulgent
> to children, are also averse to discipline. [4] Confucius, essentially a practical-
> minded statesman, saw that unless the virtue of filial submission was stressed,
> youth would be corrupted by the kindly indulgence of parents. [5] Unless
> loyalty and public service were made the cardinal virtues of the nobleman, the
> selfish interests of clan and family would prove fatal to the state. [6] The
> detached indifference with which the Chinese are prone to regard the affairs of
> the world beyond the family circle must be corrected by a firm insistence on
> the value of benevolence, submission to authority and loyal service to the
> prince.

Sample essay paragraph based on source: A

> [1] I feel that Confucianism is based on Confucius' shrewd appreciation of
> Chinese character, and seeks to lay down rules to develop it. [2] Like the
> modern reformers, Confucius deplored the particularism of the Chinese, and
> emphasised filial submission and loyalty. [3] This might seem oppressive until it
> is realised that the Chinese, a people who are naturally benevolent and
> indulgent, do not like discipline. [4–5] Confucius saw that it was important to
> stress filial submission, loyalty and public service. [6] The detached indifference
> with which the Chinese are supine to regard the rest of society must be
> improved by insisting on the value of benevolence, submission and service.

Sample essay paragraph based on source: B

> [1] One way of getting at the essentials of Confucianism is to relate it to the
> values prevalent in Chinese culture in Confucius' day. [2–4] Thus, C.P. Fitzgerald

argues that the Chinese were by nature family-centred, indifferent to the wider world of society, and not given to taking discipline; [5–6] Confucius' purpose, then, was to supply by his teaching the sense of discipline and civic responsibility that was missing from the national character.[1]

1. C.P. Fitzgerald, *China: A Short Cultural History*, London 1961, p. 88.

A close reading of these two passages from imaginary essays should show that A is a clumsy paraphrase suggesting poor understanding of the source used, and B makes a reasonable attempt to express the thought of the passage in the writer's own words, relating it as appropriate to the needs of the essay. Several points can be made in illustration of this contrast:

- Notice that example A repeats the structure of the original, sentence by sentence, trying to use different words; while B is able to stand back from the original, seeing it as a whole and commenting on it.

- Example A begins 'I feel …'; this has to mean that the imaginary student writing these words *feels*, but he is not in reality saying what he feels – he is just paraphrasing Fitzgerald's cautious suggestion that Fitzgerald is inclined to feel, and expects that most people would feel.

- Example A: 'like the reformers of today': this simply paraphrases Fitzgerald's 'Like the reformers of the modern age', without understanding of context. Fitzgerald first wrote these words even before the Chinese Communist Party was secure in power in China. Whatever reformers he meant cannot be referred to as of 'today'.

- Does the author of A understand what Fitzgerald means by 'particularism'? The clumsiness of the whole paragraph leads the reader to doubt that the writer has a good understanding of the concepts involved. It is unwise to repeat an abstract or technical term from your source where the reader might suspect that you do not understand it. Express the thought in a way that clearly shows your understanding. Passage B does a better job ('family-centred, indifferent …').

- Example A: 'supine'. An extreme case, but it can happen: the imaginary writer is anxious to change the words of the original, so looks in a thesaurus for something else that means 'prone'; unfortunately, 'supine' has completely the wrong meaning. Changing words here and there is no substitute for using words you understand to say something you really think.

- Example A: 'must be improved'. To 'correct' (Fitzgerald's word) can indeed mean to 'improve', as correcting publisher's proofs improves the script, but Fitzgerald does not mean that Chinese indifference to the interests of society as a whole should be enhanced or turned into a better sort of indifference; he means that it should be replaced, or perhaps *improved upon*, by a different set of values.

- Example A bases what is said on something that has been read, but fails to cite it. The fact that a source has been used must be acknowledged by proper citation in a footnote, as is done in B.

- Example A is generally clumsy and literal-minded, and does not demonstrate good understanding of the source; it merely paraphrases it.

- Many people (including scholars who study China) might think that because Confucianism emphasizes conformity and became established in China, this must mean that Chinese society was very conformist. Fitzgerald, however, suggests the opposite – it was precisely because it was *not* that Confucius recommended conformity, in order to enhance civic consciousness and responsibility. This is surely an interesting point of historical interpretation – in some circumstances a teaching might be evidence of its own opposite. Example B latches on to this idea: Confucius wanted to supply 'what was missing'. This shows appreciation of the underlying idea of what the source is saying.

From these examples it should be possible to see in action the contrast between paraphrasing and using independent thought.

Questions

1 Consider the complaint that it is not possible to display independent thought in an essay because the student knows so little about the subject, and the authors of the sources consulted know so much, that the student cannot say anything that is not dependent on what he has read in the sources. Compose a brief explanation in answer to this complaint, showing that a student essay can display independent thought after all. Make sure that your explanation expresses your own response to the problem and is not an unthinking repetition of anything in this chapter. (It may be best not to compose your explanation too soon after reading relevant parts of this chapter.)

2 Consider some justifications for the practice of deliberate plagiarism which you have met, or can imagine (some examples: it is legitimate because it subverts the dominant paradigm; it is a valid learning tool; it is ironic; it is a skill worth learning in its own right;

most books are full of plagiarism anyway). What do you think of these justifications? What are the pros and cons?

3 In this chapter, as on other pages here, a distinction is made between propositions in a book which should be regarded as statements of fact and others which should be regarded as expressions of views. Discuss the merits of the argument that every statement is value laden, and there are no such things as facts.

Writing and Organizing your Essay

Chapter overview

- ▶ The way in which a sentence you write appears in its context sends an implied message to the reader about its function, and you must control such messages.
- ▶ As you write, you need to make clear the structure of your developing argument, sometimes writing connecting passages or signpost sentences.
- ▶ A cool objective style is a virtue; choose your language carefully and avoid unwarranted judgments.
- ▶ Quotations must be made for a reason; the words quoted are either important evidence in their own right or need to be discussed for the purposes of your argument.
- ▶ Your concluding section needs to complete the argument neatly, showing where the discussion has led and linking it back to the question raised by the title.
- ▶ Between your own writing in the present and the actual past events you study, there are layers of evidence that you must assess critically.
- ▶ Unclear thinking about the layers of evidence can result in unclear and inaccurate writing.

After all the planning, the time comes to start the actual writing. Do not lose sight of the big picture, because every sentence of the essay must play a deliberate part in the shape of the whole. But the details are also important; every sentence must give the right message. A carelessly written sentence may tell the reader something completely wrong!

Every sentence gives a signal

As you write, each sentence sends out a signal by virtue of its placing and the way in which it is written. Learn to recognize the ways in which your sentences are giving signals.

Types of sentences

Sentences have different jobs to do. These jobs are not usually spelled out ('In this sentence I am giving some evidence which seems to be fairly reliable ...' and so on). Some sentences may combine two or more jobs, but typically each does just one. The context of the sentence and the way it is written let the reader know what job is being done.

What, then, are the different jobs?

1 *Setting the stage for discussion of a problem*: defining concepts, describing your approach, showing the meaning of the question, giving necessary background. Normally, this job is done in the introduction to the whole essay, but subsections of the essay occasionally require their own introductions. A problem is defined and explained before it is directly attacked. This introduction does not need rigorous documentation; the mere fact that citations are not attached to the statements you make sends the signal that this is introductory discussion, setting out what will thereafter be taken for granted, before embarking on the analysis of evidence. Once the direct attack on a problem begins, the documentation must be rigorous.

    This sort of sentence means: 'This is introductory; it sets the stage for what follows. I propose to take these facts for granted, or to adopt these definitions of concepts, for the sake of argument.'

2 *Presenting evidence in the form of information*: stating evidence which can be treated as reliable for your purpose. (See Chapter 6, 'Distinguishing between factual evidence and judgment or opinion'.) A sentence which presents such evidence should do so in your own words and carry a footnote for each use of a source.

    This sort of sentence means: 'This is what I have found out and I am treating it as factual evidence. I know no reason for distrusting it. The evidence I am using is all in the sources cited, which I have inspected myself.'

3 *Identifying an idea, judgment or inference attributed to a historian*: referring to possibly debatable statements derived from secondary or tertiary sources. If you know that somebody disagrees with them, or can think of possible criticisms, you must treat them as opinion or interpretation, not as factual evidence. Say what historian expressed what idea, and attach a citation. (If you do not mention or cite your source, you are signalling that the idea presented is your own; this would be plagiarism.)

    This sort of sentence means: 'I am taking this historian, named in the citation, as my authority, and this (in my own words) is what he thinks.'

4 *Saying things which represent your own independent thought*: saying what you independently think. Such a sentence must be supported by evidence already described, or about to be described.

This sort of sentence means: 'These are my own words. This is what I think. The evidence for it is already stated, or about to be stated.'

5 *Quoting from a source*: repeating exact words from what you have read. Any quotation must be identified by inverted commas (quotation marks) or indenting, and must have a citation of its source. The justification for quoting is that the words quoted matter to your discussion.

This sort of sentence means: 'These words are a quotation (documented in the footnote) worth noticing particularly because their precise meaning matters to my argument.'

6 *Citation*: citing the source on which information or an idea mentioned in the essay is based. The citation appears either in parentheses in the text or in a note.

It signals: 'This is where I found it. You can verify it.'

Make sure that the logical structure is plain

An essay question requires answers; answers require reasoning; reasoning requires documented evidence. The reader must see clearly how these are all linked. An essay is not successful if a good argument is merely hinted at or implicit in it. The material must be clearly identified and properly articulated. Sometimes, it helps to offer strategically placed *signposts* at the transitions between different stages of the argument.

Transitions and signposts: the beginning of each paragraph generally marks a transition from one idea to the next. The first sentence of the paragraph should ideally be crafted to hook neatly on to the previous paragraph, showing the connection between the thought of each. If you try too hard to do this, the result may look childish; this must be avoided. Do not write things like:

In the previous paragraph we looked at the second reason. Now we will look at the third.

You can, however, incorporate a *signpost sentence*, one which makes clear what you are doing and introduces the subject matter of the next section:

In order to decide whether industrial conditions can be described as bad, first we need to examine the evidence about rural workers.

What, then, were the forms taken by the persecution of Christians? Let us turn to ...

These are the two conflicting views; which is more convincing? The case for the first is that ...

Avoiding bias in your writing

We have already considered this in your reading (in Chapter 6, pp. 57–61, 'Tendentious or disputatious language'). You must avoid bias or tendentiousness in your own writing as well as recognize it in the writing of others.

Be as objective as possible. Whatever you feel about the question under discussion, let that feeling be embodied in the cogency of the argument, rather than in the colour of the language. Some issues arouse strong feeling. Of course, there is room for passion in history. But a passionate conviction is most likely to persuade the uncommitted when argued coolly and rationally. An essay is an exercise in the proper use of rational argument, and must persuade by reason and evidence; nothing more. Yet, it is much more absolute, more telling, more irresistible if it succeeds with a studious neutrality of language than if it loads every phrase with a charge of judgment. It is then most likely to convert a critical reader to your view.

Do not build gratuitous judgments into your language. Expressions such as this will not do:

'With unashamed rapacity, the French then set about ...'

If you feel strongly that something in the empire-building of the French deserves to be condemned, you must first be sure that your evidence compels condemnation. If you are sure, simply set out coolly the evidence that compelled you. Your conclusion will be all the more damning for its lucid objectivity.

Quotations

When is it useful to copy out passages word for word in your notes? It is useful when you may wish to include such passages as quotations in your essay. (See Chapter 7, p. 65, 'When to write out quotations'.) When you write up the essay, you need to decide finally what passages to quote word for word.

Do not use quotations too often. This is dangerous. A quotation may be an honest alternative to plagiarism, but it is not a substitute for your own words, your reflection on what you have read. It is usually better to summarize what a source says than to quote it. The main substance of an essay is the writer's own ideas, and passages from sources are not his ideas.

Normally, quote only when you wish to discuss the words quoted. The chief legitimate occasions for quotations are these:

1 *A primary source*: What a primary source says is often worth quoting. It will provide the most telling sort of evidence for the argument. Quoting it can show that the author is interpreting it correctly, not misrepresenting it; words from the horse's mouth are the most convincing. Be sure to clarify what the connection is between the quotation and the argument that you are presenting.
2 *A historiographical discussion*: When you are discussing what different historians have written about an obscure or contentious topic, it is often desirable to quote what they say in order to be sure of representing accurately their points of view. Interpreting what they said may require fine distinctions, and then it is best to give the reader the words they used, thereby supporting your interpretation.

Writing the conclusion

An essay is a work of art; it is not something that can be put together, like a model aeroplane, by mechanical observance of instructions. Nevertheless, if your muse does not give you confident guidance, there is a lot to be said for that cliché of the schoolroom, the instruction to write a concluding paragraph which sums up what you have said and links it to the original question.

Try, though, to do it elegantly. Do not sum up by plodding laboriously through the stages of an argument that should have been clear enough already; your summary should be revelation rather than repetition. Indeed, you may recapitulate briefly the essential points from what has gone before, but chiefly you will wish to show, not what has already been spelled out, but where it has all led.

Try to distil the essence of your argument in a way that adds one final thought – a thought that grows out of what you have just been saying without repeating it, and which makes the last neat link with the original question in the title. This helps the reader to see the engineering in the construction. The essay is good or bad only to the extent that it succeeds in answering the question; the conclusion, then, should be like the keystone in the arch that adds the last indispensable element to the structure.

The conclusion should focus on some point that expresses your own independent thought. If the essay question asks you to account for some event, and you identify several factors which can be seen as contributing to the event, you must explain and justify your own position on the importance of these factors. Avoid the sort of fence-sitting answer you might give by merely identifying some possible explanations *without saying which you think are the most important.*

If you do not attempt to rate the importance of different factors, you abdicate independent thought. You must attempt some analysis of the relative importance of the factors you consider, even if the result of the analysis is not fully decisive. The conclusion will round out the discussion by showing what you make of it all.

Matching words to ideas

Errors may result from unclear thought or ignorance. Those that result from unclear thought are much more numerous than you may think. If the underlying thought in an essay is confused, the confusion will work through into the choice of words, the grammar, the spelling, the punctuation and all aspects of the style. Thus, it happens very often that a student writes clumsy and ill-expressed sentences, with various errors of English in them, not because of ignorance of the principles of English expression, but simply because of confusion about the subject matter.

You need to examine every sentence that gives you the slightest qualm. Exactly what is the thought behind it? What are the things talked about in the sentence, and what are the relationships between those things? What sorts of things are they anyway – people in the past, things written a long time ago about people in the past, or books about the things written about people in the past? Sometimes, when you can get these categories and relationships straight, the problems of style and grammar may solve themselves.

Consider this sentence:

> The sources of the terrorists' motivations do not give much information about problems for the interpretations made by scholars to solve.

If you look carefully at this sentence, it will probably seem somehow wrong. But how, exactly? The sentence juggles with the concepts of 'sources', 'motivations' and 'problems'. These concepts refer to things on different levels which must not be confused. In particular, the use of the word 'sources' in this sentence is confusing. Should the writer have written 'causes' instead of 'sources', or does he actually mean to refer in some way to sources in the historical sense – documents which the historian can read and use?

Below is a table showing *different levels* on which the ingredients of history belong. You must decide *what are the categories* whose relationship you wish to describe, to what levels they belong, and what is the actual relationship between them. The table is arranged archaeologically, with the raw material of history, the original causes of things that happened in the past, at the bottom, and you at the top. As you look at history, you search downward through layers of evidence towards the elusive truth below. If you are to see clearly, you must identify and label each layer, and be able to describe accurately how something from one layer is related to something from another. Generally speaking, in this table, each item depends on or is made possible by the one below it.

Elements coming between historical processes and the student who wishes to write about them
10 Your essay
9 Your thought about the problems of understanding your sources
8 Problems of interpretation raised by the secondary and tertiary sources
7 Secondary and tertiary sources
6 The ideas of the writers of the secondary and tertiary sources
5 Problems of interpretation raised by the primary sources
4 Primary sources – documentary evidence
3 Observations of events, from which primary sources come
2 Historical events and behaviour
1 Causes of historical events, motives of behaviour

In history, we find all manner of actions and events which we want to understand. We do not know very well what the causes of these actions and events were, but we want to find out. At any rate, we can say that the events and actions are to be explained by *something*, are caused by something, and whatever causes things to happen goes at *level 1*. All the other things that affect our study arise from it.

At *level 2*, we find the actual events and behaviour. For history, even if not for philosophy, we take it for granted that some particular real events and behaviour actually happened in the past, and that when we know about them we can, within the limits of our evidence, accurately describe them.

However, we cannot observe these things with our own eyes. We depend on observations made by people living at the time, or good information received by such people, who could then write down what they thought they knew. These observations are at *level 3*.

The observations in turn make possible the writing down of accounts which contain information, however inaccurate or distorted, about the historical events. These are our primary sources – *level 4*.

We must study these sources, but we must also study the problems raised by the possible inaccuracies and distortions; in an important sense, these problems engender the debate and conflicting evidence which are at the heart of historical research – *level 5*.

The existence of these problems attracts people to study them. These people develop their own interpretations – *level 6*.

The interpretations then form the basis for what they write in books and articles, which are secondary sources. The secondary sources attract other people to write other things on the basis of them, and these other things are tertiary sources – *level 7*.

The secondary and tertiary sources contain different ideas, because there is no finality to the solution of historical problems. The interpretations differ, which creates problems for the student – *level 8*.

The student has then to engage in close study of the problems by examining all the available sources – *level 9*.

This study makes possible the writing of an essay – *level 10*.

Now we can look at the ill-expressed sentence that was taken above as an example, and see how it should be analysed in the light of this table.

The first part of the sentence states: 'The sources of the terrorists' motivations do not give much information …' What does not give much information? Scholars need to obtain their information from sources, and the most basic sources are primary ones – the things written by the terrorists themselves, or by people who knew them. Primary sources are on level 4 – documentary evidence. The writer is confusing this with level 1, on which are the sources of behaviour, so these two levels must be kept apart. The writer means to say, perhaps, that the documentary evidence available about the terrorists' motivations is not very helpful, being too thin.

The second part of the sentence states that the 'information' mentioned is 'about problems for the interpretations made by scholars to solve'. The information desired is what is looked for in the primary sources, level 4. This, the writer thinks, is unsatisfactory, and it certainly raises problems (level 5), as well as being *about* problems of behaviour, or the problems which the terrorists wished to solve (which has to do with their original motivation, level 1). The interpretations made by scholars (level 6) are applied to the problems (level 5). The solutions to the problems are not, strictly speaking, made by the interpretations (level 6); they are made by the scholars themselves, or, by extension, by the things the scholars wrote (level 7).

The writer of the defective sentence had not properly sorted out these relationships, and thus confused documentary evidence with sources of behaviour, and scholarly interpretations with scholars or their writings. When these distinctions of level are all clear, it is possible to see better how the sentence might be written:

> The documentary evidence available to shed light on the terrorists' motivations is inadequate, and does not furnish enough material for scholars to solve the problems in accounting for the terrorists' actions.

What all this shows is that it is essential to adjust the focus of your vision to the layers of cause and effect that you see as you look down towards historical truth, to sort out clearly which is which, and to choose the right words to express the relationships between them. If your thought is confused, you will make avoidable errors of expression. If it is not confused, you will be able to attend directly to writing accurate English.

Questions

1 In the light of the table above showing the elements intervening between original historical circumstances and the essayist writing about them, rewrite the following rather confused sentence, which is based on the example of the five skeletons found in the Indus Valley site discussed in Chapter 6:

> The evidence of the five skeletons found in the city changes the sources for the later writings, which originally wanted to prove that the city did not collapse until the five people were killed.

2 In what ways is the writing of an essay a work of art? In what ways is it a piece of engineering?

12

Citing the Sources

Chapter overview

▶ What you write counts as academic only if you make it easy for the reader to check your evidence.

▶ When you present evidence, you need to supply information about your source so that it can be checked.

▶ As soon as you start discussing the evidence, you need to start giving this sort of information.

▶ The way in which the information is presented should conform to a system to make sure that it is adequate.

▶ There are two main sorts of system: (a) identifying the source in your text, and (b) using notes and bibliography.

▶ Type (a) works better for scientific studies, (b) for humanities, especially history, which needs the footnotes as a place for further discussion of sources.

▶ Notes do their job when they can be easily noticed by the reader, not when they are hidden away.

▶ The use of ibid. many times in immediate succession gives the impression of lazy essay construction.

▶ You must always have sighted whatever source you cite.

Academic writing needs verifiability. For verification, there must be *documentation* – proper citations. The first section here concerns the question of which statements need support by the citation of sources. The following sections concern the details of citations.

What needs a citation?

You cannot provide citations for *everything* you write. In practice, historians put citations in the places where they feel intuitively that citations are required, usually getting it right without thinking about any rules.

So how do we decide where citations are needed? Sometimes it is said that citations are needed for information which might be new to the reader, but not where the information is obvious, but this will not solve all problems. Here is the beginning of an imaginary essay under the title: 'How do you account for the rise of Buddhism in India?':

> The Buddha is generally considered to have been born in the sixth century BC. At that time a cosmopolitan urban society was flourishing in the capitals of rising states.

There are no citations here. Is this because the statements are all obvious, and the reader is likely to know them? But consider the following from an imaginary essay written to the title: 'When did the Buddha live?'

> The Buddha is generally considered to have been born in the sixth century BC.[1] However, the question has recently been reopened by Bechert and others.[2]

Here the first sentence is unchanged, yet it has documentation. Why? Is it any less obvious than in the first case? The explanation is that it is not the degree of obviousness that counts. It is the *relationship between the statement and the argument of the essay.*

Consider the first case. The sentence appears in an introductory paragraph that is setting the scene, describing the background to the rise of Buddhism. For this purpose, it does not matter exactly when the Buddha was born. The substance of the argument has not begun. Once it gets under way, there will be documentation. In the introduction, however, the facts stated are *those that can be taken for granted for the purpose of the essay.* Citations are not called for.

In the second case, the same sentence is performing a different function. It is now dealing directly with the answer to the question set. We must not take for granted anything about the date of the Buddha. If people generally think the date was the sixth century BC, we need to *question the evidence* for this. What is it? Citations are needed.

What matters is *whether the writer intends to take for granted the truth of a statement for the purpose of discussion, or needs to call it into question.* In the introduction you are setting the scene, showing what things are relevant but can be taken for granted for the purpose of the discussion. After that, a threshold will be crossed, and every statement will be made only because it contributes to the answer to the question set. The earlier absence of citations is in itself a signal that the scene is still being set; documentation signals that the argument is now under way.

What, then, is rigorous documentation? It is documentation of everything you write that depends on material derived from your sources, whether you are treating it as fact or as opinion. If your argument does not depend on it, do not mention it. If your argument does depend on it, you must document it.

It may seem that this system needs far too many footnotes. However, in practice, many paragraphs will be occupied with your own observations, and you will find that not many pages require fatiguingly dense citations.

Giving references

Citations are made by inserting the information needed to identify the particular sources used. This enables the reader to check the sources and the way in which they are used.

There are various citation systems. Some require information in parentheses *in the text* (sometimes called 'in-text' citations) and some require it *in notes* (sometimes called 'note-bibliography' citations). The note comes either at the foot of the page or in a list on a later page. Notes in general are often called 'footnotes', wherever they occur, but often the word 'footnote' is reserved for those at the foot of the page, and those grouped together later are called 'endnotes' (at the end of an essay, chapter, article or whole book). Practices vary.

Here are preliminary examples of the in-text method and the note-bibliography method:

1 In-text method

> ... and this view is advanced by J. Smith in his recent study (Smith 2014, 127).

Here, the writer makes a statement based on something on page 127 of a work by J. Smith published in 2014. Smith's work is identified by author and date. This enables the reader to turn to the bibliography and find the entry for a work by J. Smith published in 2014. The bibliography entry gives complete information, so that the reader may then find the original source in order to check up.

Sometimes, in-text citation systems name only the author, not the date of publication: 'Smith 127'.

2 Note-bibliography method

> ... and this view is advanced by J. Smith in his recent study.[1]

> 1. J. Smith, *A Short History of New Zealand*, London, 2000, p. 127

Here, an indicator number appears at the end of the sentence where the source is used. The corresponding number appears at the foot of the page, introducing the note, which contains all the information needed to track the source down. But if the same work has already been cited on earlier pages, the footnote need not repeat all this information; a suitable abbreviated format can be used. The bibliography will supply full details.

Documentation is governed by the rules laid down by various systems; you have to learn the rules of the system used. It is altogether probable (although not certain) that you will have a particular system prescribed for your use in essays. Nevertheless, details of the main types of system in use are offered below. It is desirable for you to have an understanding of the ways in which different systems work; this will help you to develop intuitive knowledge of the purposes and nature of documentation conventions and prepare you for the different systems you will encounter in your reading and also in your future writing as a student or an author.

Sections on the in-text method and the note-bibliography method follow below, with particular attention to the MLA and Chicago styles. The Chicago style wisely favours in-text formats for scientific writing and note-bibliography for writing in the humanities, including history. However, students of history have various systems of documentation prescribed for them, and sometimes these have in-text formats. On general grounds, as we shall notice further below, the note-bibliography format is better for history. Nevertherless, we shall review some features of both types of format. For the reasons just noted, it is good to be familiar with various systems.

You may already know that you will be required to use one particular system, and save reading about the details listed below until later.

In-text citation systems

The MLA documentation system

This system requires minimal detail in the text. For a full account, see J. Gibaldi, ed., *MLA Handbook for Writers of Research Papers,* 7th edn (New York: MLA), 2009.

What appears in the text: in parentheses, author's surname and page:

(Smith 127)

If the bibliography contains more than one entry under 'Smith', identify the one concerned:

(Smith, John 127)

If the bibliography contains more than one work by the same Smith, identify the one concerned by using a short form of the title:

In his earlier work, Smith expressed this view (*Short History* 127), but in a later article he reported a change of mind ('Reconsideration' 424).

There is no footnote; the reader must turn to the end of the chapter, book or article to obtain complete details from the list of sources. This list may be headed *Bibliography,* especially in a book; in an article or chapter it is more likely to be headed *References* or *Works cited.* In what follows, bibliography will be preferred.

Bibliography

Each bibliography entry is placed in strict alphabetical order, ignoring spaces between words. 'Vanbrugh' comes **before** 'Van Loon', 'Saint John' **before** St Benedict.

Book with single author: surname; initials or personal name; title in italics; place; publisher; date:

> McManners, John. *The French Revolution and the Church.* London: SPCK Publications, 1969.

Notice the punctuation, which is part of the prescription.

Where there are two or more works by one author, use three hyphens and a full stop (period) instead of repeating the name:

> McManners, John. *The French Revolution and the Church.* London: SPCK Publications, 1969.

> ———. *Death and Enlightenment: Changing Attitudes to Death among Christians and Unbelievers in Eighteenth-century France.* Oxford: Oxford UP, 1981.

For more than three authors or editors, name the first and follow with '*et al.*' ('and others'):

> Desai, Meghnad, *et al.,* eds. *Agrarian Power and Agricultural Productivity in South Asia.* Delhi and New York: Oxford University Press, 1984.

In a bibliography, but not in a footnote, the first author in an entry is named surname first; for more authors, the others with initial or personal name first ('Smith, J. and Raymond Brown'). Include initials, personal name or a combination according to what appears in the publication (on the title page, if it is a book). Omit titles of rank etc.; include forms which distinguish people of the same name (write 'Smith, John III'; 'Smith, John Jr'; **but not** 'Smith, Brigadier Sir John'). Reproduce the whole title, normally with a colon before the subtitle.

Compilation/anthology: editor's/translator's/compiler's name; role in relation to book; title; place; publisher; date:

> Young, Alfred E., ed. *The American Revolution: Explorations in the History of American Radicalism.* De Kalb: Northern Illinois UP, 1976.

Chapter or article in a collection: name of author; title of item in quotation marks/inverted commas; title of book; role of editor/translator/compiler;

name of editor/translator/compiler; place of publication; publisher; date; first and last page numbers:

> Hut, Piet. 'Conclusion: Life as a Laboratory.' *Buddhism and Science: Breaking New Ground.* Ed. B. Alan Wallace. New York: Columbia University Press, 2003, 399–415.

Article in a reference book: name of author; title of item; title of reference work; 'ed.' or 'eds'; name of editor or editors; number of volumes if more than one; place of publication; publisher; date; page numbers:

> Quinton, Anthony. 'British Philosophy.' *The Encyclopaedia of Philosophy.* Ed.-in-Chief Paul Edwards. New York: The Free Press. Vol. 1.

If the reference work is well established (such as the *Encyclopaedia Britannica*), the name of the editor, the place of publication and the publisher may be omitted, and the number of the edition inserted.

Article in a learned journal: author's name; title of article; title of journal; volume number; date; pages:

> Sen, Raj Kumar. 'Taxation principles during Kautilya's age.' *Indian Economic Journal* 37 (1962): 133–8.

Omit 'The' from the beginning of the name of a journal. If the volume has a continuous pagination sequence throughout, you need not include the issue numbers or the season. If you cite from a magazine, this may not be so. If there are separate pagination sequences for issues, they need to be identified:

> *Kansas Quarterly* 13.3–4 (1998): 17–45.

Issues 3 and 4 of volume 13 were published together with a single pagination sequence running through both.

Chicago Manual of Style

Here, briefly, are examples illustrating the widely used *Chicago Manual of Style* documentation format: *The Chicago Manual of Style*, 16th edn (Chicago: University of Chicago Press), 2010. It specifies an in-text system for the sciences (author-date), and a note-bibliography system for the arts, literature and history. For reasons already noted, both will be described here. Chicago's author-date style, unlike the MLA, **uses the date as an essential item** for identification of a publication. For scientists, the date of an article may be important, but history students also may sometimes be asked to use citation systems with this feature.

Author-date style – book with one author:

> *In bibliography*: McManners, John. 1969. *The French Revolution and the Church.* London: SPCK Publications.

> *In text:* (McManners 1969)

Notice the placement of the date in the bibliography.

Author-date style – journal article with one author:

In bibliography: Sen, Raj Kumar. 1962. Taxation principles during Kautilya's age. *Indian Economic Journal* 37: 133–8.

In text: (Sen 1962, 136) *or* (Sen 1962).

Notice that quotation marks/inverted commas are not used around article titles. Also note that optionally the actual page used in the journal article may be included in the reference in the text.

Footnotes

From this point we shall be concentrating on the note-bibliography style. The previous section ended with the *Chicago Manual of Style* system using the in-text method; for the arts, literature and history the Chicago system prescribes the use of notes.

Chicago note-bibliography style – book with one author:

In bibliography: McManners, John. *The French Revolution and the Church.* London: SPCK Publications, 1969.

In footnote: John McManners. *The French Revolution and the Church.* (London: SPCK Publications, 1969).

Notice the use of parentheses in the note but not the bibliography. Also, as expected, the surname comes first in the bibliography but later in the footnote.

Chicago note-bibliography style – journal article with one author:

In bibliography: Sen, Raj Kumar. 'Taxation principles during Kautilya's age.' *Indian Economic Journal* 37 (1962): 133–8.

In footnote: Raj Kumar Sen. 'Taxation principles during Kautilya's age.' *Indian Economic Journal* 37 (1962): 136.

Notice the use of quotation marks (inverted commas) around the article title. The bibliography identifies the first and last page numbers, while the footnote identifies the particular page containing material used from the source.

Turabian

Widely used is a handbook by Kate Turabian with guidelines covering all aspects of documentation and presentation. It has been through multiple editions brought out in coordination with the editions of the *Chicago Manual of Style*. There is an eighth edition: Kate L. Turabian, *A Manual for Writers of Research Papers, Theses, and Dissertations*, revised by

Wayne C. Booth, Gregory G. Colomb, Joseph M. Williams, and the University of Chicago Press Editorial Staff (Chicago: University of Chicago Press), 2013.

Footnote citation in history

In the arts, literature and history, adherence to published codes such as the MLA and Chicago is not quite as firmly established as in the sciences. Publishers frequently do not prescribe a published system. They do, however, require that, whatever style of documentation the author uses, it should be *consistently applied*. This is essential. Stick to your system's rules; do not combine it with any other.

Where does the footnote indicator number go?

The footnote number goes above the line at the end of the appropriate phrase, clause, sentence or paragraph of text embodying the use of the source. It goes *after* most punctuation, inside a closing parenthesis if the statement requiring documentation is within the parentheses, and outside if the statement documented is outside:

> Few writers would nowadays subscribe to this opinion (although Smith, in a recent article, gives it qualified support[1]).

> Most recent writers spend little time on this argument (or even ignore it altogether).[1]

The footnote number necessarily goes at the *end* of any quotation:

> As Smith wrote, 'The Conte process revolutionized pencil manufacture.'[1]

Generally, it comes at the end of a sentence, except where the use of the source is embodied only in an earlier part of the sentence, the later part serving some different purpose:

> The inscription offers exhortations to piety rather than laws,[1] so we may wonder how far these inscriptions really had the nature of laws.

Footnoting conventions

Here, some conventions will be described. They are commonly observed in the literature of the humanities (the arts or the liberal arts generally), but do not apply in all standard citation systems. For example, you may have noticed that the MLA and the Chicago systems described above use full stops/periods between items of information in a citation, and do not use abbreviations like 'p.' and 'pp.' for 'page' and 'pages'; practice in the humanities has much use for commas and abbreviations. You might find:

London, 2000; London, OUP, 2000; (London: OUP), 2000; (London, OUP), 2000 – but only one method in one book.

Citing a book

In the note, name these: the author or authors (initials or personal name first, then surname); the full title (in italics); the place and year of publication, together in parentheses (the publisher's name may not be required); the page or pages (abbreviated as 'p.' for one page, 'pp.', for more than one). Alternatively, the publisher may be named also and the year given outside the parentheses. For subsequent references to the same work, see below.

> J. Flood, *The Riches of Ancient Australia* (St Lucia, 1990), pp. 48–57.

Alternatively, the publisher may be named also:

> J. Flood, *The Riches of Ancient Australia* (St Lucia: University of Queensland Press), 1990, pp. 48–57.

Points to notice:

1 Notice 'p.' for one page, 'pp.' for more than one, *not* 'pg' or 'pgs'.
2 If there are more than three authors or editors, use the expression *et al.* ('and others').
3 The place of publication should be the name of the *town* (or suburb) as usually given on the back (sometimes front) of the title page. **It should *not* be the state, county or country.** Thus: 'Harmondsworth', not 'Middlesex' or 'UK'; 'Englewood Cliffs NJ', *not* 'New Jersey' or 'USA'.
4 Capitalize consistently. One principle is to use *maximum* capitalization in a title (all nouns, verbs and adjectives). Some systems use minimal capitalization: for the first word in the title and proper names only.
5 It is good practice to be as helpful as possible to the reader. Thus, you can name the publisher as well as the place of publication. (The major standard citation systems generally require this anyway.)
6 Essays are nowadays normally written on computers. You can observe the printer's convention of using italics for the name of a book or journal, foreign words, subheadings and so on. In handwritten work, underlining is used for these purposes.

Citing a journal article

Name the following: the author or authors, initials first (but surname first in the bibliography); article title in single inverted commas (quotation marks); journal title, in italics; its volume number (in Roman or Arabic as prescribed, or as found in your source, but be consistent); the part or number of the volume (although this is not essential unless each part has its own pagination sequence); the date (but not the place) of publication, in parentheses; the first and last pages. (For subsequent references to the same work, see below.) Two examples:

> A.J.P. Taylor, 'Progress and Poverty in Britain, 1780–1850', *History*, vol. XIV (1960), p. 16.

> R. Bellah, K. Burridge and R. Robertson, 'Responses to Louis Dumont's *A modified view of our origins: the Christian beginnings of modern individualism*', *Religion*, vol. 12 no. 2 (April 1982), pp. 83–8 at p. 87.

Points to notice:

1 Observe that the two examples above do not follow exactly the same conventions. The first uses maximum capitalization in an article title, the second uses minimum capitalization.
2 The second identifies the issue of the journal as the second for the year, published in April. This is not mandatory, if a single sequence of page numbers runs through the whole volume. The alternative would be: vol. 12 (1982), pp. 83–8 at p. 87.
3 The second places the article within the volume by naming the first and last page numbers, *and also* identifies the particular page from which the reference was taken. This is not regular practice and is rarely prescribed, but it can help the reader.
4 In the second example, notice the use of italics to identify a book title, even within the title of an article (which itself is marked by inverted commas).

Citing an edited book

When a book consists of edited material, refer to it as to a book, using the name(s) of the editor(s) in place of an author, followed by 'ed.' or 'eds', as appropriate. Then proceed as for any other book:

> Peter Amann (ed.), *The Eighteenth Century: French or Western?* (Boston, 1966), p. ix.

Points to notice:

1 Here, the reference is to something the editor has written. Editors often write introductions to material by others that they have edited, and sometimes introductions have small roman pagination, as here.
2 If the material edited consists of work by just one author, the book should normally be cited under the author's name. To refer to something written by the editor in his introduction, adopt the format: J. Smith, 'Introduction', in T. Brown, *The Story of My Life* (London, 2000), p. ix.

Citing a chapter in an edited book

Many edited books consist of multiple articles or chapters by different people. To refer to a chapter in such a book, give the name of the author and the title of the chapter (as though for a journal), followed by the citation of the book as above:

> R.F. Smith, 'Drink in Old Russia', in E.J. Hobsbawm *et al.* (eds), *Peasants in History: Essays in Honour of Daniel Thorner* (Calcutta, 1980), p. 47.

Citing an item in a documentary collection

To refer to an item in a published collection of documents, cite the document itself, followed by the book in which it is published:

> Disraeli to Lady Bradford, 23rd Oct. 1877, in Marquis of Zetland (ed.), *The Letters of Disraeli to Lady Bradford and Lady Chesterfield,* vol. II, 1876–1881 (London, 1929), pp. 142–3.

> John of Salisbury, *Policraticus*, trans. J. Dickinson, in J.B. Ross and M.M. McLaughlin (eds), *The Portable Mediaeval Reader* (Harmondsworth, 1977), pp. 251–2.

Abbreviations	
f.	following page
ff.	following pages. However, it is normally recommended that you should give the actual numbers of the last pages concerned; i.e., pp. 44–5 rather than 44f.; pp. 44–51 rather than 44ff.; in the latter case, there is unwanted vagueness
ibid.	(= *ibidem*) 'in the same place'; i.e., in the same work previously cited – immediately before, usually in the preceding footnote. *Ibid.* identifies the previous citation even if on the previous page. '*Ibid.*' saves you the trouble of writing out the last citation again, except for the page number if it is different. If it is not different, there is no need to repeat the page number
idem	'the same person'; instead of repeating the name of the author just mentioned in the previous reference
loc. cit.	(= *loco citato*) 'in the place cited'. This functions like *op. cit.*, but in reference to articles or documents within a book rather than to a whole book. This abbreviation is now not often used
op. cit.	(= *opere citato*) 'in the work cited' (by the author named). This saves you the trouble of writing out again a citation of a work you have already noted within the previous two or three notes
p.	page (not pg.)
passim	here and there; i.e. at scattered points throughout the passage
pp.	pages

Citing a work already referred to

If your previous reference to the same work was the one immediately before, use *ibid.*, as indicated above. If it occurred in the last two or three notes, use *op. cit.* for a book, *loc. cit.* for an article. Many publications use *op. cit.* for previous references however far back they were made, but this is not recommended. To find the full citation, the reader has to hunt back through the book, checking every footnote, to the first mention of the work.

Therefore, for a second or subsequent reference to a work, give the author's surname and a convenient *short version* of the title, enough to indicate what sort of source it is and make it easy to identify it in the bibliography. If your essay does not refer to any other work by the same author, the author's name alone may be sufficient to identify the reference.

Journal titles can be abbreviated from the start; they usually have standard abbreviations anyway. Examples include:

AHR   *American Historical Review*

EHR   *English Historical Review*

Econ.HR   *Economic History Review*

JAS   *Journal of Asian Studies*

A sample series of footnotes:

1. Benjamin Quarles, *The Negro in the Making of America* (New York, 1964), *passim.*

2. R.H. Hilton, 'Mediaeval market towns', *Past and Present*, No. 109 (Nov. 1975), p. 9.

3. Quarles, pp. 81–2.

4. Hilton, p. 16

    ....

21. Quarles, *The Negro*, pp. 81–2.

22. Hilton, 'Market towns', p. 16.

Notice that in the last two notes the titles are repeated, in short form, because in each case the first reference occurred more than a couple of notes ago, and the reader needs more clues to the nature of the source.

What sort of citation style suits history?

Any citation system that allows the writer to identify sources adequately for verification may be good enough. Beyond that, the merits of the details are not vital to successful practice of history. It is nevertheless important to master them and use them consistently, following a clear and appropriate system. This is because:

- when the accurate use of your citation system has become second nature, you will be able to use it easily thereafter, without making mistakes
- you will have the habit of thoroughness that will be invaluable later when you prepare materials for publication.

Once you have mastered a citation system, you will be able to keep your mind on the problems of argument and conflicting evidence. Nevertheless, some comments are worth making.

In-text versus note-bibliography systems

In-text citation, although originally adapted to scientific disciplines, has spread to many others, often including history. However, for various reasons, although it can be adapted for history by the use of abbreviations, footnotes are preferable. In-text citation systems imply that most of their objects will be published works with authors or editors and dates of publication. History, however, seeks to use any sources whatsoever, in as great a variety as possible; if they are unpublished primary sources, all the better. Further, the in-text method has a built-in assumption that citations of sources need not be accompanied by discussion of the problems of interpreting the sources cited, and can therefore dispense with footnotes. For history, however, footnotes are often necessary to accommodate further discussion of the sources used.

For the historian, it matters what sort of source is being cited at each point; there is no assumption that passages cited contain hard information raising no problems of interpretation. The reader needs to know, from a glance at the citation, whether the source is primary, secondary, or tertiary, and preferably more besides. As much as possible of this information should be there on the page; the reader should not need continually to turn to other pages.

Footnotes and endnotes: Whether you put your notes at the foot of each page or at the end of the essay may be prescribed for you. Given a choice, put footnotes on the page. The reader, if seriously anxious to assess what you write, will wish to see, wherever there is a footnote, *what sort of source you have used*. This requires that the actual note should be immediately visible.

Computers make it easy to put footnotes on the page, and this is much better. In published works the same applies, yet it is strange that sometimes academic books require the reader desiring to consult an 'endnote' to go on a complicated chase. It is the notes that provide the evidence for everything the writer says, giving constant clues to the quality of his research.

Text in footnotes

Some disciplines prefer evidence that can be taken at face value. Statistics from a government office can commonly be taken for granted as accurate by an economist, who does not feel a need to keep turning aside from his analysis to assess critically the way in which the statistics have been collected. By contrast, the historian's sources require to be assessed critically at every point.

The historian operates on two levels – identifying and assessing evidence, and discussing its significance when its value is assessed. Discussion of the interpretation of the sources, on points of detail, may often be best separated and placed in footnotes, so as not to interrupt the flow of the argument. So footnotes may often be used to discuss the interpretation of the sources, while the main argument is carried forward in the text.

Here is a commonplace example, from S.F. Bemis, *The Hussey-Cumberland Mission and American Independence*, Princeton, 1931, p. 74:

> 17 Cumberland's No. 8 to Hillsborough. See Appendix No. 9. Observe that Floridablanca's note ascribes to Cumberland himself the initiative in the matter of setting down thoughts on paper, in the interview of June 21.

What can go in a footnote?

This question is succinctly answered by some good advice from Turabian:[1]

> Notes have four main uses: (a) to cite the authority for statements in text – specific facts or opinions as well as exact quotations; (b) to make cross-references; (c) to make incidental comments on, to amplify or to qualify textual discussion – in short, to provide a place for material the writer deems worthwhile to include but that might interrupt the flow of thought if introduced into the text; and (d) to make acknowledgments.

Here, (c) encompasses the features of footnotes that have just been discussed. Two more categories could be added:

1 Text of a quotation in the original language when a translation appears on the page above (or a translation, when the text appears on the page above).

2 Explanation of allusions. Where the text mentions some name of a person or institution, a technical term, or some concept being used in an unfamiliar way, a footnote may be the place to show that you

understand what it means – that you are not just repeating what a source says (plagiarizing it) without independent thought.

Good and bad footnoting

Avoid using ibid too often

Repeated reference to a single source is rarely justifiable. It may be justified in an essay studying a particular primary text, which may need to be cited in many successive notes (although the essay as a whole must be enriched by discussion based on other sources).

Exceptionally, in one section of the essay there may be only one source that can be used. Keep such sections short.

Generally, however, a string of *ibids* creates the immediate impression that the essay is lazily constructed by relying too much on one source, or by using a number but simply summarizing them one at a time, without making the effort to collate and compare the evidence and ideas from different places.

Where one source is unavoidably cited quite a few times in succession, economize on footnoting by letting one note at the end of a paragraph do duty for the contents of that paragraph. It should identify all the pages of the book used in the paragraph, perhaps using *passim*.

You must sight what you cite

Citation of a source carries with it the signal that you have obtained the evidence of the fact by *looking at* the source cited. Therefore, the source must be one which you have inspected yourself, not merely read about. If the original source X is accessible to you, and what it says is important to your argument, you should inspect it for yourself and cite it directly. Always cite the best sources available for your purpose.

However, when all else fails, if a documentary source is important to your argument and needs to be cited, but is not available to you except as cited by somebody else, you may wish to cite it as in this example:

> 1. *The Rig Veda*, Book X.VI, stanzas 3–4, cited by J. Smith, *History of Indian Literature* (London, 1933), p. 16.

Bibliography

You may be asked to supply with your essay a critical bibliography. This should exhibit as wide a range of sources as possible. Your teacher may look at it first, before starting to read the essay, to gain an impression of the research that has gone into it. Include everything that has helped you write the essay, whether it is cited anywhere in your text or not. Do not include anything that has not helped at all, even if you have read it.

The more works you have read, the better the feel you will have for the subject. Each source offers its own approach to problems, perspectives, points of view, sources of evidence, helping you to develop independent thought and judgment as you review and compare. Therefore, a long bibliography is preferable to a short one.

Arrange your bibliography in alphabetical order of authors. Place the author's surname before initials. This is in contrast to the footnotes, where initials or personal names come first. Sometimes, particularly in US usage, personal names are preferred to initials. Alternatively, initials may be required, or there may be no prescribed form, in which case it may be best to follow the form in which the author's name appears at the head of the work, but with surname first.

In other respects, cite the works in full, exactly as in their first occurrence in a footnote; identify the first and last pages of an article (there is no need to specify what individual pages you have used within this range).

Your bibliography may benefit from being organized into sections, each with its subheading and alphabetical sequence; the most generally useful division is into primary and secondary sources.

Annotation

If your bibliography is required to be critical, this means that it must have annotations commenting on the use you have made of each item. You can add either a few phrases or a few lines of comment to each item, or alternatively consolidate your comments into a short bibliographical essay at the end, using half a page or so to deal with the list as a whole. For example: 'Smith and Brown were useful in giving general background; Jones drew my attention to the debate about the importance of ...; Robinson provided detailed evidence of ...' .

These annotations are not (as in secondary sources or textbooks) to guide the reader's further study but to show your teacher quickly what value you have derived from each source and whether you have seen clearly in what way it is relevant to the topic. Your critical comment should not say how good or bad you think each work is (unless there is some reason for remarking on its particular strengths or weaknesses); it should say in what specific way it was of use. If it was of no use, do not include it.

The importance of citation

So much, then, for the technicalities of citation. The subject cannot be presented without a wealth of details. One might be forgiven a moment of impatience: is all this detail really important?

What justifies it is that in the end it is all-important to adhere to the standard of *verifiability*. Only then is your writing properly academic. Verifiability requires all the information needed for verification, and detailed rules can help maintain a high standard of verifiability.

Remember too that you may in future prepare material for publication. This job leaves no room for sloppiness – all the tiny details must be standardized. So, right at the beginning, acquire the habit of taking care over these details. Professional standards demand precision.

To learn any skill – to play tennis, lay bricks, speak Swahili, design office blocks or anything else – it is necessary to spend time at the beginning learning painstakingly the details of preferred practice. Later on, the rules can be followed effortlessly and you can concentrate much more closely on the difficult and interesting bits.

Questions

1 What, in general, are the pros and cons of in-text noting systems as against those of note-bibliography ones? Which, if either, do you prefer, and why?

2 What are the particular characteristics of history as a discipline which affect the desirability of one type of noting system rather than the other?

3 Do you think it is a good idea for a student to have a reasonable familiarity with different noting systems? Why?

The Importance of Good English Expression

Chapter overview

▶ Do not hesitate to take appropriate advice on how to improve your written English – from your teacher, a remedial English tutor, or appropriate books.

▶ It is extremely wise to avoid writing essays with so many mistakes in English expression that the person who has to mark them becomes irritated.

▶ Mispunctuation is a frequent flaw in essay writing and deserves particularly close attention.

▶ A history essay is literature, and requires the characteristics of literature, avoiding note form, jargon, colloquialisms, excessive division under subheadings, excessive use of quotation, sloppy grammar or poor final checking.

Before an essay is submitted, it needs to be checked carefully for style and expression as well as content and documentation. This chapter is concerned especially with accuracy in written English. Many of the statements that follow may look somewhat arbitrary and dogmatic, but in matters of accuracy there is a thin line between what is right and what is wrong. English expression has to be accurate to make your prose easy to read. Careful learning in the early stages yields benefits later.

If you still need convincing that English expression is relevant to writing history essays, think about these points:

● Numerous errors distract and irritate the reader, especially a reader who has to correct the essay, and they mar the impact of what you have to say.

● Clumsy writing actually obscures the meaning; history writing must be precise and clear, so vagueness and obscurity are serious defects.

- Since there is no clear line to be drawn between a historical thought and the expression of it, a badly expressed essay is a badly thought essay.

One qualification: many of the rules below may sometimes be breached legitimately by competent writers. They are, nevertheless, stated here dogmatically. Knowing when they can be breached legitimately requires an assured mastery of style and sensitivity to the nuances of register and idiom. You need to prove that you understand all the rules properly before you can claim the privilege of breaking them!

Accuracy of English expression

Accurate English expression is not to be regarded as merely the icing on the cake of a good history essay. It is more like the flour in the cake. English writing and history writing are not two different activities. There is only one activity.

First, some pieces of practical advice:

1 To repeat a point which was made above, it is good practice to keep a dictionary in reach while writing, and check the spelling and meaning of all doubtful words. A dictionary installed in your computer cannot be relied upon for everything. It will not tell you about shades of meaning, and it cannot identify misspellings when they correspond to other words which exist but which you did not mean. Also, bear in mind that the spelling of many English words is different in different countries.

2 You may well benefit from reading a manual dedicated to the problems of expression in student writing, such as Gordon Taylor's *A Student's Writing Guide: How to Plan and Write Successful Essays* (Cambridge: CUP), 2009.

3 *Mispunctuation* is perhaps the most ubiquitous form of error. Make sure that every sentence is properly constructed.

4 Do not use *abbreviations* in your essay. Your teacher is entitled to use them in his corrections, because these are notes; abbreviations belong to notes, not to literature, and your essay is literature.

Sometimes, students' experience with history can bring to light problems best dealt with by consulting specialists in remedial English tuition. If you find that you need help with your expression, you may do well to seek such assistance. If not, consult specialist English composition manuals. What follows here is no more than a list of reminders. They start from the most basic and technical, and work up to questions of style.

Punctuation

Commas

A single comma must not intervene between subject and verb, or between verb and object or complement. Two commas, however, may intervene – at the beginning and end of an inserted phrase or clause:

> Philip tried with all his might to prosecute the counter-reformation effectively in the Netherlands.

or:

> Philip tried, with all his might, to prosecute the counter-reformation effectively in the Netherlands.

But not:

> Philip tried, with all his might to prosecute the counter-reformation effectively in the Netherlands.

and not:

> Philip tried with all his might, to prosecute the counter-reformation effectively in the Netherlands.

NB: You need to be aware of the difference in meaning between the two following cases (and see below, in the section on 'relative pronouns'):

> All the Netherlanders, who preferred Protestantism, were mercilessly persecuted.

> All the Netherlanders who preferred Protestantism were mercilessly persecuted.

Sometimes, commas are used to separate items that are presented in a list (Smith, Brown, Jones, Robinson …). A comma is not needed between the last item and the last but one if the items are single words or short phrases ('Smith, Brown, Jones and Robinson' – although some people prefer to include one), but is certainly needed if the items are long:

> Woollen garments, felt, steel goods and glass mirrors were exported from Europe in this period.

> The ruler succeeded in driving his kingdom into economic ruin, alienating nearly all of his subjects, forfeiting the goodwill of monarchs throughout Europe, and bringing the country to the brink of war.

Commas may be used between clauses where the second is introduced by a conjunction. If there is no conjunction, the two clauses are separate sentences and must be divided by a full stop (period) or a semi-colon. An adverb cannot be used to join them. Here are some examples:

Lincoln's cause is nowadays regarded as right because he won, but history would not make the same judgment if he had lost.

or:

Lincoln's cause is nowadays regarded as right because he won. However, history would not make the same judgment if he had lost.

or:

Lincoln's cause is nowadays regarded as right because he won; however, history would not make the same judgment if he had lost.

But not:

Lincoln's cause is nowadays regarded as right because he won, however history would not make the same judgment if he had lost.

and not:

Lincoln's cause is nowadays regarded as right because he won, however, history would not make the same judgment if he had lost.

Semi-colons

Syntactically, semi-colons are used where full stops (periods) would also be correct. They are not used where commas or colons would be correct. Some examples:

Where a head of state is succeeded by a member of his immediate family, the principle of monarchy is at work, even if the relative does not succeed immediately.

and not:

Where a head of state is succeeded by a member of his immediate family, the principle of monarchy is at work; even if the relative does not succeed immediately.

Caesar finally arrived on English soil; he saw that there was a good opportunity for further conquest.

and not:

Caesar finally arrived on English soil, he saw that there was a good opportunity for further conquest.

Colons

Syntactically, what follows a colon extends, or is in apposition to, a substantive which precedes it. What follows the colon should be a substantive, or a list of substantives, or quoted words in inverted commas, which as a whole constitute a substantive. It identifies with detail what is constituted by the substantive that precedes:

What the Prince wanted was the comforts of a convivial weekend: good companionship, ladies of style and charm, good drink, and many decks of cards. [Here, 'comforts' is the substantive to which the noun phrases after the colon stand in apposition.]

and not:

What the Prince wanted was: good companionship, ladies of style and charm, good drink, and many decks of cards.

Parentheses

Parentheses enclose any punctuation belonging to the text within them. If they enclose a question, the question mark goes inside the closing parenthesis. Punctuation belonging to the encompassing sentence goes outside the closing parenthesis. It does *not* go before the opening parenthesis:

Wellington generally had a positive attitude to his troops (although on a famous occasion he said, 'They may not frighten the enemy, but by God they frighten me!'), and this goes far to explain his success.

Square brackets

Unlike parentheses, square brackets are used to include explanatory editorial matter inserted within a text, usually within the text of a quotation, to indicate that the words inserted are not part of the quotation:

As the governor unwisely put it, 'In all social systems, a *sine qua non* [essential element] of the structure is a class to do the menial duties, to perform the drudgery of life, requiring but a low order of intellect.'

Full stops (British usage) or periods (US usage)

Full stops/periods divide clauses that are not joined by conjunctions, for these are separate sentences. Strictly speaking, they must not be used to divide units that lack main verbs, for, in theory at least, every sentence must have a main verb:

I came. I saw. I conquered.

I came, I saw, I conquered. [This is legitimate as the successive items are a *list* of parallel constructions.]

and not:

Even though the residents of Boston and Cambridge were accustomed to the sight of ex-soldiers, whose experiences in the war seemed to set them apart as a separate species of beings, who saw the world quite differently from their neighbours.

However, the definition of a sentence (by its possession of a main verb) is blurred by the fact that, in practice, many types of phrases or individual words may be left out or *understood*, especially in colloquial but also in relatively formal speech. Therefore, a full stop may conclude a seemingly *verbless sentence*:

> So far so good. We may yet win. Perhaps so. Perhaps not.

Apostrophes

Apostrophes must not be put in any places where they are not needed (for example, nouns which end in vowels do not as a rule form their plurals with apostrophes):

> It's an irony of history; its irony was not lost; the smith's forge; the smiths' forges; the sheep's fleece; the sheep's fleeces; the children's quarters; potatoes and tomatoes; in the 1950s; the Visigoths invaded; the Habsburgs' empire; Wilberforce's campaign; the manifesto's contents; the theses' seditiousness; the 95 theses.

Italics

Titles of literary works need to be in italics, but not the titles of articles or chapters within them. So do terms in foreign languages. In the following citation of an imaginary article, notice that the name of a journal is what constitutes the title of the work:

> J. Gardner, 'The Use of the Term *Volk* in Hitler's *Mein Kampf'*, *Journal of German History*, vol. CCLXI (2000), pp. 1–20.

Terms in foreign languages are italicized. Many words of foreign origin have been adopted with infinite tolerance into the English language, and are normally used without any sense that they are foreign – for example 'rendezvous', 'per se' (especially in America), 'wallah', 'angst', 'liaison' (which also prompted the adoption of the back-formation 'liaise' in armed services slang, formerly requiring inverted commas in literary use but now widely accepted as a word), 'role'. Other words are less often used, and sometimes italicized (*'prima facie'*/'prima facie', *'Weltanschauung'*/'Weltanschauung'). You are at liberty to italicize any such word which is sometimes used in English, as a sign that you recognize it as foreign, but if you do this too much it will look precious. Remember that, if you are treating a particular word as foreign by putting it in italics, it must have the appropriate diacritics, capitalization, etc. ('*Angst*', not '*angst*'; *rôle*, not *role*).

In handwriting, the use of underlining matches the use of italics in print.

Spelling

The only way of avoiding spelling mistakes is to consult a dictionary whenever necessary. If you have a blind spot for spelling, you are in good company – many of the best people, masters of prose in other respects, have the same problem. Make sure that you always have a good dictionary at hand. The bigger the dictionary, the better. From a source like the *Oxford English Dictionary*, or even the *Shorter Oxford English Dictionary*, you can learn a great deal about the origins and history of words as well as how to spell them.

British and US standards: there are two main spelling standards, British and American. For example, Australia mainly follows the British, although with some American spellings widely followed also (chiefly 'or' endings for 'our', as in 'color' and 'favor', and 'program' for 'programme').

Grammar

Main verb

Every sentence must have a main verb (except as noted above). Do not lose track of the syntax of a long sentence – it must be properly controlled, with a main clause in the right place.

The following passage, intended by its (imaginary) writer as a sentence, lacks a main verb and is therefore not a properly constructed sentence:

> At the time of the defeat of Spain, when the American colonial regime was instituted, although it was made clear that the intention was to prepare the Philippines for eventual independence.

Agreement

The number of the verb must agree with the number of the subject. This is easily lost sight of when the two are widely separated. The following sentence fails to preserve subject-verb agreement and, strictly speaking, is wrong:

> The ferocity and ruthlessness with which the Conquistadores set about crushing the unprepared local population is among the most striking features of the period.

Tension between grammatical form and intended meaning

This last example, however, points our attention towards an area of uncertainty. Do the words 'ferocity and ruthlessness' identify a single entity? They do not. Ferocity and ruthlessness are different things, here claimed to be conjoined in the behaviour of the Conquistadores. They demand a plural verb. A singular verb will seem quite wrong in a sentence such as 'His ferocity and ruthlessness is amazing.'

On the other hand, noun phrases of plural form do sometimes identify genuinely singular entities, chiefly sums of money and names ('Three guineas is exorbitant'; *Great Expectations* is a tale brilliantly told'; 'Johnston, Soames and Harbottle is a well-respected legal firm'). There are also borderline cases where a speaker or writer uses words which identify a plurality of different things but intends them as a label for a single idea; consider the sentence 'Law and order is our most pressing concern'. Here, the cliché 'law and order' might be argued to be justifiable as singular. If so, the justification would be that 'law and order' is a cliché, a formula to denote a recognized single concept.

Tense

It is often tempting to switch tense for literary effect in a narrative. This must be handled with care, however. A deliberate change of tense at a particular point for a particular purpose is one thing; random inconsistency in the use of tenses is another, and is to be avoided. The following passage has an improper change of tense:

> The news came when he was playing bowls. He was quite determined to finish his game before acting. On arrival in London, he immediately seeks to find out all he can about the invading fleet, and forms his plans for dealing with it.

Parallel constructions

Grammatical parallels are a frequent source of error. The elements treated in parallel must be a syntactical match for each other:

> The trial of Dreyfus was both a miscarriage of justice and a milestone in the course of modern social history.

and not:

> The trial of Dreyfus was both a miscarriage of justice and came to be regarded as a milestone in the course of modern social history.

In the latter example, 'a miscarriage of justice' is a noun phrase, and therefore not a proper parallel for its companion, 'came to be regarded ...' which is a predicate.

Personal pronouns

Be careful with the agreement of number between pronoun and noun. (Do not use 'it' where 'they' is required, and vice versa.)

The indefinite 'one' should not be replaced by 'he' on subsequent occasions; the word 'one' should be repeated:

> One will soon discover that one's prejudices were wildly off the mark.

> *and not:*

> One will soon discover that his prejudices were wildly off the mark.

The words 'he', 'him', 'his' and 'himself', and 'man' or the compounded '-man' are used to refer either to males only (as masculine pronouns), or to people in general (as pronouns of common gender), and which is intended should be apparent from the context. In recent years, many people have taken to restricting their use of these words to the masculine gender, and finding other ways of referring to people in general. Whichever practice you choose, it is essential to be consistent.

If you choose to use these words with either masculine or common gender, according to context, avoid the possibility of confusion. In cases where the reader might wonder whether you mean males only or people in general, choose an alternative form of expression that is not ambiguous:

> Every male soldier who entered a building was required to remove his cap.

> All soldiers, male and female, were required to remove their caps on entering a building.

> *and not (if in the context there is an ambiguity):*

> Every soldier was required to remove his cap on entering any building.

If you choose to use these words with masculine gender only:

- *Avoid inconsistency*: If you begin a series of references to people in general with 'he or she' or 'him or her', you cannot later switch to a simple 'he' or 'she'.

- *Avoid clumsiness*: 'Him or her' repeated within a sentence can be very clumsy and awkward, and on further repetition becomes ridiculous; another way of expressing the thought should be found.

- *Avoid confusion*: The following examples show how the attempt to avoid common gender 'he' and so on can lead to ambiguity.

> Anybody who makes prolonged attempts to come to terms with the ideas in books by historians influenced by such writers as Derrida and Foucault will find that they are lost in obscurity. [Who are the people lost in obscurity – writers

such as those named, historians influenced by them, the books they write, the ideas in the books, or the person who makes prolonged attempts?]

A person wanting genealogical information should consult the local history teachers and their close relatives.

Defining relative pronouns

'Laziness, and laziness alone, was the besetting fault which thwarted his ambitions.'

Should the writer have used 'that' instead of 'which'? In this sentence, the relative clause 'which thwarted his ambitions' defines and restricts the application of the antecedent 'fault'. The choice of relative pronoun in a defining relative clause is sometimes seen as an issue. Many regard it as a rule of grammar that 'that' should always be used, not 'who' or 'which'. In 1926 Fowler in *Modern English Usage* argued eloquently for this practice; it was a reasonable recommendation, but as he acknowledged it was not a rule. Nor is it a rule now. Many writers, familiar with the arguments, continue to prefer 'who' or 'which' because it sounds right, and they prefer to adhere to the rule that 'who', not 'which' or 'that', should be applied to a person, as in the following sentence:

Any woman who agreed to marry Henry VIII needed to have supreme indifference to her own fate.

Handling quotations

Spelling

In quotations, always use whatever spelling is in the original. Do not change from American to British or vice versa, or modernize, or correct – although if the error is just a trivial misprint with no conceivable reason why the author should have intended it, there is no harm in making the correction.

Sic

If you are quoting a passage in which there is a mistake which might have been intended by the original author out of ignorance (not just a trivial misprint), it should be reproduced, and you can signal that this is the author's own original mistake, not yours, by using the word *sic* ('thus'). The signal given by *sic* is: 'this is in the original. I am not responsible for it.'

Some writers use *sic,* not to signal apparent mistakes that were in the original, but to convey an attitude of ridicule and derision (as if to say, 'Yes! Fatuous though it may seem, he actually wrote this!'). Avoid this practice.

Syntax of quotations

If what is quoted consists of or begins with a complete sentence, it may be introduced by an appropriate verb ('says', 'said', 'declared' etc.), followed by a comma. If it consists of or begins with a syntactically incomplete sentence, the words which introduce it must combine with it to form a syntactically complete sentence; any punctuation before the opening inverted commas must be whatever punctuation is required, if any, by the syntax of the sentence thus formed.

Here is an example from a student essay which illustrates what not to do. It comes from a passage about the Koran:

> Similarly one should '... praise of thy Lord before sunrise and before sunset.'

Clearly, the word 'praise' in the quotation is being used as a noun, and therefore cannot function in the whole sentence as a verb. The error could be removed by introducing the quotation with the words: 'Similarly one should offer'

Sometimes, the punctuation before the opening inverted commas should be a colon. An example is in the last sentence of the previous paragraph. The quotation with which the sentence ends is in apposition to the word 'words'.

Where you can see no way of incorporating the quotation into a syntactically complete sentence without modifying it in some way, show that you are making a modification. Three dots represent an omission, and square brackets indicate something you are putting in, whether to complete the syntax or to make clear what is being referred to:

> As indeed Smith has argued, the new discoveries '... [go] far towards showing that [Brown's] theory must now be completely rejected.'

If you quote a complete sentence, presumably the original began with a capital letter, but the first word of the quotation may not be at the beginning of a sentence in your essay, and you may wish to change the capital to lower case. Similarly, a quoted incomplete sentence may, on occasion, require a capital when it appears at the beginning of your sentence. In each case, it is legitimate to make the change. Some writers signal that they are making the change by enclosing the transformed letter in square brackets. This is not necessary.

Style

Note form

Abbreviations are for notes, and perhaps for technical reports, but not for literature. An essay is literature, and should not use note form. Certain abbreviations are indeed recommended in the footnotes (as described above), but they should not be used in the text.

There are, to some extent, exceptions. 'Etc.' ('and the rest'), 'i.e.' ('that is') and 'e.g.' ('for example') may be allowed, used sparingly, or may be disallowed altogether. Do not use a large 'C' for 'century' ('Luther lived in the C16').

Note form is represented by abbreviations and other techniques to save the labour of writing standard literary prose, such as leaving out words that are required by the syntax but can be understood, and using characters other than standard letters and numerals. The solidus '/' can normally be replaced by 'or'. Many writers favour the use of 'and/or', but it is best avoided. If further precision is needed, add 'or both' later in the sentence ('His failure to guard against this was evidence of carelessness, or stupidity, or both'.)

Avoid jargon and colloquialisms

Write in standard English. This is what will be understood, written and aspired to by people from any English-speaking country, whatever their dialect or accent, by people who are not native English speakers but have been well taught, or by people who have not lived in an English-speaking country for many years. There is a blurred boundary zone where experts disagree about what counts as standard.

Some words or expressions may be well established in academic writing and have good authority behind them but not be familiar to everybody simply because they are rare. These can be used, but not to show off, and not if a simpler expression can be used with exactly the same meaning. Occasionally, it may be desirable to use some technical term of recent coinage that has not long been in general use:

> Marxism brought in a new paradigm for the study of history.

Here, 'paradigm', as applied to fields of scholarly study, has come recently to mean more than its basic sense ('model', 'standard'); following the writing of Thomas Kuhn on the sciences, it has become popular as a term implying the theory that, in each branch of scholarly study, from time to time, with advancing knowledge, the framework of assumptions about the basic character of the field becomes impossible to sustain and a new set of basic principles, or paradigm, has to be developed.

Many words of relatively recent coinage which help to give a racy tone in more informal sorts of writing are unlikely to be universally understood and do not belong in standard formal English. Others are well established in conversational English and widely known, but are colloquialisms nevertheless, and not to be used in standard formal written English – 'guy', meaning 'man' or 'person' in an indefinite sense, is an example, as is 'OK'.

Subheadings and lists

It is useful in setting out a report, and frequently in a textbook or handbook such as this book, to help the reader to see the arrangement and sequence of the content by using many headings and subheadings (or even sub-subheadings), and by presenting material in lists of items.

An essay is not, however, the same thing as a report, a textbook or a manual. As a rule, the prose should not be broken up into parcels. Some parcelling may be in order, but not much. The most that is likely to be acceptable is the division of your essay into a small number of sections, with headings.

An objection to breaking up the prose of an essay is that it may point the student in the wrong direction. As you write, you should regard your prose as a single argument in answer to a single question, a seamless web of reasoning which accommodates the evidence which is specifically relevant and proceeds directly to demonstrate the conclusions. If it is broken up into pieces, this encourages you to lose sight of its essentially unitary structure and treat it as a series of collections of information, like a report.

This need not happen, however. So long as your prose genuinely retains the character of an essay, subheadings can be useful in performing the same function as signpost sentences, indicating the transitions in the stages of the argument and keeping its shape before your eye, or that of the reader.

Similarly, it may occasionally happen that a list of items, arranged in a series of (perhaps indented) paragraphs marked with numbers, letters or bullets, may help to set out your material economically. If you wish to refer to a significant number (more than three) of theories about a historical subject, or pieces of evidence which must be considered, and wish to say something but not much about each, an itemized list may be right.

The danger here, though, is that, having presented a list, you may forget to offer your own thought about the subject. A list of other people's theories is no substitute for what you consider yourself. If you give a list of other people's ideas, you must then proceed to discuss them critically.

If you wish to provide yourself with a guide to the shape of your argument, you need not write subheadings – you can prepare a synopsis, setting out in note form the plan of the argument. If you wish to provide your reader with such a guide, you can present the synopsis with your essay. (Academic journals often require authors to supply synopses or 'abstracts'.) Some teachers might welcome it, as an exercise in getting your own purposes clear and in showing them at a glance how you have executed them.

Avoid woolliness, pomposity and padding

This particularly afflicts introductory sections, but can contaminate a whole essay. It is usually a sign that the writer does not understand very well what is required of an essay, and tries despairingly to imitate what strikes him as the abstract, polysyllabic style required by scholarly writing. Alternatively, it is a sign that he thinks he is going to write a two-volume book on the subject, and feels obliged to begin by discussing what the question means at great length.

You should be able to avoid this. Keep in mind just what the question requires and exactly what you are going to do in order to satisfy that requirement. In the introduction, write in simple straightforward language just what is needed to show the reader how you see your job and how you are going about it. There is no need to be sidetracked into explanations that are not going to affect your subsequent argument.

Questions

1 How much do you think correct grammar matters? Justify your answer, referring to examples of practice considered good by some and bad by others.

2 'I before E except after C.' This is a rule-of-thumb guideline for remembering how to spell certain words containing 'ie' or 'ei', which often but not always works. Have you learned any such useful guidelines for remembering tricky points of grammar, spelling or punctuation which deserve to be shared? If so, what are they?

3 What do you think are the particular features of the English language that are likely to make it more easy, or more difficult, for non-English speakers to learn?

Revision and Correction

Chapter overview

► The chapter is short and consists of numerous distinct sections with checklists and subheadings; a brief scan of the pages will quickly indicate its content.

► It is about the culminating stages in the life of an essay, during which you may derive maximum educational benefit from the whole exercise. In particular, learn as much as you can from the corrections and comments. It will be of interest to notice the grade awarded, but in the long run you may gain more from taking trouble to understand the criticisms in detail and acting on this understanding in later work.

The final preparation of an essay requires certain steps, especially the following:

● Ensuring that the essay is of appropriate length and fulfils the formal requirements laid down.

● Careful checking of all the information that must go into footnotes and bibliography, with missing details hunted down and included.

● Rereading to make sure that the argument is clear and economically presented.

● Word-by-word scanning of the entire contents to eliminate all errors, especially errors in English.

The task of revising is least stressful when little alteration is required. To achieve this, the right steps must be taken before writing starts. Careful planning will enable you to produce a draft that attends succinctly and economically to the question addressed. Then you can realistically attend to these basic principles:

1 The result must be as nearly perfect as possible.
2 The final draft must be attractive and a pleasure to read.

Some principles of revision

Leave your essay to lie fallow for as long as possible

Ideally, you should leave plenty of time before the deadline so that you can forget about your essay for a while and then come back to it with fresh eyes. It is difficult to detect faults in recent writing. After time has passed, though, you begin to recognize the repetition, obscurity, inadequate reasoning and missing argument, as well as the slips of the pen or misprints which are so difficult to pick up.

Use computer tools cautiously

Computer word-processing programs often come with their own dictionaries, which can check for spelling mistakes or misprints. This is useful for proof-reading, but will not remove the need to be able to write English accurately or use a real dictionary. Computer grammar-checking tools have limited use and may mislead; you must be your own grammarian.

Do not revise on the computer screen

The best way to revise an essay composed on a computer is to print it out and make the revisions on paper. The changes can later be transferred to the digital version.

On a printed page, most people find, it is much easier to recognize mistakes. You can shift your glance instantaneously between footnotes and relevant text. Further, you can quickly and easily scribble in provisional or experimental changes, and cross out some of them, before deciding on final revisions.

Edit by cutting out, not putting in

Sometimes, you may need to write more in order to provide necessary evidence or spell out a weakly reasoned argument. Nevertheless, you are more likely to make big improvements when you omit some passages. Aim to produce a lean, spare essay. Cutting out unnecessary fragments here and there throughout may be surprisingly effective. Ask yourself rigorously whether each section, paragraph and sentence is really necessary; be prepared to make ruthless sacrifices when the answer is no.

Get help from a friend or colleague

Of course, if somebody else actually writes or plans parts of your essay, that is plagiarism. However, within limits, it may be appropriate to have somebody else read through your draft and draw your attention to points at which improvements are possible. Such a person, reading with fresh eyes, may see better than you can where there are slips and errors of expression, and places where the argument is not clear and needs more explanation. You must take full responsibility for everything in the final draft, but you may take another's comments as stimuli to make improvements.

Layout and presentation

The suggestions below are recommendations you can follow unless they differ from what is prescribed for you.

The title

The full title must be accurately written out at the beginning. This is more important than you may think. On the correctness of the title, the whole fate of the essay depends, for your essay succeeds only to the extent that *it succeeds in answering exactly the question with which you begin*. No amount of assiduous research or intelligent writing will avail if it does not answer the question which is actually set. The title at the beginning of the essay, every word in place, must govern your thinking as you plan and write.

Length

Observe the prescribed length. Part of the craft of writing is to say what is important within specified limits. If you write significantly more or less than is prescribed, your essay may lose points, and the latter portions of an excessively long essay may be ignored for marking purposes. Word-processing programs normally have word-counting tools; these count all words, including footnotes and bibliography.

Legibility

Features of format will probably be prescribed – for example, double spacing and wide margins. These facilitate corrections. Choose a clear unfussy font with serifs. Avoid handwritten corrections.

Page format

Use a standard paper size (e.g. A4 or 8.5" x 11" in the US), and use one side only. Number the pages; the teacher may wish to use these numbers for his comments.

If such details are not prescribed, it is important to leave a good margin especially on the left side of each page. It should be wide enough for any corrections and comments, probably 1.5 inches or 4cm, excluding any holes, binding or plastic strips.

Footnotes

If there is a choice, prefer *footnotes* to *endnotes,* for the excellent reasons described in Chapter 12. If *endnotes* are prescribed, they should be easily separable from the text pages (clipped rather than stapled).

Numbers

Numbers can be written either in words or figures. Where standards are formally prescribed, they commonly require that numbers up to ten should be in words, and higher numbers should be in figures. (NB: In literary contexts, especially in direct speech, numbers high or low are often in words. The choice is partly influenced by context. Where the writer's purpose is to discuss quantities, figures are clearly required; where it is to emphasize an idea rather than a quantity, words may be preferred.)

Second copy

Make sure you back up your paper, both in electronic form and in hard copy; the back-up copy must be unchanged from the version actually submitted.

A checklist of revision points

Fundamental matters, such as the underlying quality of thought and argument, have been discussed in earlier chapters. The lists below contain mostly technical details.

Use of sources

- Evidence properly identified and distinguished from interpretation or judgment
- Evidence properly documented
- Authority for interpretations or judgments properly acknowledged
- Best available evidence consulted, especially primary sources. Internet sources used only if reliable as academic authority or useful primary source evidence
- Authorities' judgments or interpretations not treated as if they were fact
- No paraphrase of authorities' words except where unavoidable in brief statements of factual evidence
- No copying out of authorities' words except in properly set out quotations
- Quotations aptly chosen to exploit primary sources or identify interpretations to be discussed
- Quotations properly set out, documented and integrated into syntax of text
- Allusions properly explained

Construction

- Proper introduction setting out plan of attack
- Ambiguous terms or concepts analysed where appropriate
- Stages of argument clearly signalled
- Concluding section showing how question has been answered

Format and presentation

- Full title at the beginning
- Length within prescribed limits
- Clear layout
- Page format: adequate margins, page numbers, indented paragraphs

Footnotes

- All material evidence documented
- No avoidable strings of *ibids*
- Footnotes all citing sources you have actually inspected, not seen cited elsewhere
- Citation format exactly as prescribed, with adequate information for verification (place and date of publication, initials, etc.)
- Unwanted data not included
- Exact page numbers given
- Abbreviations properly used (*op. cit., ibid.* etc.)

Accuracy of language

- Clarity
- Succinctness – cull all unnecessary passages
- Abbreviations not used
- Note form not used
- Colloquialisms not used
- No woolly, pompous sentences that say nothing important
- Every sentence expressed as simply as possible
- All words used accurately with full knowledge of their meaning; no malapropisms
- Avoidance of awkward clumsy phrasing
- No use of prejudicial, tendentious language
- Correct punctuation and spelling
- Correct grammar

Bibliography

- Bibliography well laid out, surnames first
- All prescribed data in right sequence
- Annotations supplied, with comment on use made of each item (not how good you think it is); justify use of any internet sites

A proof-reading exercise

Below is a sample of bad writing, with many errors in the English or the format. It illustrates common sorts of mistakes. This sort of exercise can be useful in reminding you of some of the things requiring attention during revision.

The passage is an extract from an imaginary essay written to the title: 'What did Hsuan-tsang achieve?' All the mistakes are technical ones embodied in particular words, phrases and so on. You are not expected to criticize the underlying quality of the argument.

1 Hsuan-tsang essay
2 Hsuan-tsang, otherwise known as Tripitaka, was born
3 towards the end of the 6th c. in China. When he grew
4 up, he concieved a powerful ambition in the aspiration
5 of purefying Chinese Buddhism, and, without getting
6 permission from the emperor he set off to find Buddhist
7 texts in India. There, he spent several years' of study among the
8 bhiksu's.
9 Buddhism in China was not a new phenomena, however
10 it's teachings had been variously interpreted and had lost
11 their pristine homogeniety. What Hsuan-tsang wanted to
12 do was to find authentic Buddhist texts in India that
13 would serve as a criteria for the reform of the faith
14 in China, and the ones he brought back, constituting a
15 very important contribution to Chinese knowledge of the
16 sacred Buddhist cannon, was carried to China on the
17 backs of 23 mules.[1] Jones[2] says that Hsuan-tsang's
18 achievement as a translator, 'the work of many year's
19 after his return, which marked a great moment in the
20 history of Chinese Buddhist scholarship.'
21 1. J. Smith, 'History of Buddhism,' Gt Britain,
22 (Macmillan), 1990.
23 2. Jones, 'The Life of Hsuan-tsang,' USA p. 17.

Corrections: 'sp.' = spelling, 'gr' = grammar, 'p' = punctuation

1 The full title should be written out, showing exactly what the question is
2 'otherwise known' – by whom? Why? What is the significance of this name?
3 'sixth century' – write out number in full, and avoid abbreviations
4 sp: 'conceived'
5 gr: 'ambition to purify'
5 sp: 'purify'

5/6 p: 'without getting permission from the emperor' is an insertion between conjunction and subject, so should have a comma before *and* after it

7 p: years

8 p: *bhiksus* – apostrophes are not used to mark plurals (NB: This could be regarded as a common technical term and left plain, but as a foreign word it could be italicized)

9 gr: 'phenomenon' – singular

9 gr/p: 'However' – beginning a new sentence. 'However' is not a conjunction here

10 p: 'its' – it is surprising how often this slip is made

11 sp: 'homogeneity'

13 gr: 'criterion' – Greek singular

16 sp: 'canon'

16 gr: 'were' – subject is 'ones'

17 documentation format: indicator should go at end of sentence stating what Jones says, not after his name

18 gr: quotation is not integrated into syntax of sentence

18 p: 'years'

21 documentation format: titles should be underlined or italicized

21 documentation format: there is no need to name the publisher, but the town (London, Basingstoke etc.) should be named, not the country

22 documentation format: page number should be included

23 documentation format: as for footnote 1

Benefiting from conferring about corrections

After the essay is revised and submitted, the process is not all over. One of the most important stages still remains – the consultation which follows correction.

You can learn much from any sort of conferring about your work, including discussing an essay with fellow students. Collaborative exchange of ideas can be extremely valuable and can stimulate your thought.

You may be provided with a statement of the marking criteria used by the teachers where you study. Such a statement will repay study – it will enable you to identify the particular aspects of your essay that will be probingly assessed.

But it is from your teacher that you can perhaps learn most, because after all your teacher is the professional supposed to be able to identify the ways in which your essay falls short of perfection and explain them to you so that you can make improvements. Only by studying and understanding the corrections can you actually learn and improve.

If you are convinced that the grade you receive is seriously wrong, consult urgently and go through whatever procedures are laid down. Here, though, the concern is not with questions of justice and rights but with ways of benefiting from consultation. If your teacher seems to you not to have understood what you were doing, or not to have identified properly what was wrong, you still need to consider carefully what made him think as he did; perhaps he misunderstood some aspect of the essay but, if it had been perfectly lucid, this would not have happened. Reread the essay and think what might make somebody see it as saying unconvincing or erroneous things, even though you did not mean them.

Make sure that you understand all the corrections. Your teacher's response to your essay is the crucible of intellectual encounter; take every opportunity to benefit from it.

If the corrections use *abbreviations,* these need to be understood. That they are used is a sign that they are frequently needed, and therefore that they identify besetting errors deserving attention. Most of the abbreviations used in correction will probably refer to errors of English, especially in punctuation, spelling and grammar.

Other criticisms of content may concern various sorts of errors in presenting the argument – 'expression poor or clumsy', 'needs rephrasing'; 'expression unclear'; 'oversimple'; 'wrong tense of verb', and so on.

Common errors

The following types of error commonly occur. If you can understand them and successfully guard against them, you can practically guarantee to score more points.

Teachers might write the following comments on student essays:

1 Evidence stated without documentation.
2 Inferences or judgments stated without evidence presented.
3 A historian's views stated and documented but treated naively as if they were the writer's, or as if they were factual evidence.
4 It is unclear how this fits into the structure of the argument. A signpost is needed to indicate how it fits in at this point.
5 Passage is unclear. Probably the underlying thought is unclear. Writer needs to make sure the reader understands exactly what is meant.
6 Explain allusions. The reference to this term, concept or name leaves doubt as to whether the writer understands it.

7 Bibliography not critical. There should be an indication of the use made of each item. (Bibliographies are often not required to have annotations, but where they are, the annotations can serve a useful purpose.)
8 Footnote reference incomplete or not in proper format.
9 Margins should be wider, leaving ample room for comments.

Questions

1 How would you describe the limit on the amount of help that an essay writer can receive from somebody else before the help given counts as plagiarism?

2 What do you think of the principle that the marks given for an essay should be the sum of a number of separate marks given for different aspects of the essay, such as English expression, originality, apt use of evidence, etc.? Is it better that a single 'holistic' mark should be awarded, combining more or less intuitive allocations of credit to the different aspects?

Beyond the History Essay

Chapter overview

- ► Examinations test not only factual knowledge but also a broad understanding of the field of study.
- ► 'Open book' examinations allow you to take in reference books, so you suffer less anxiety about failure of memory, but they may also encourage undue focus on looking up facts rather than reflection on interpretations.
- ► 'Short answer' questions have limited use in history; 'multiple choice' questions have practically none.
- ► Examination conditions demand intense mindfulness and careful thought about what the examiners will be seeking in your answers.
- ► Document criticism exercises focus attention narrowly on specific primary source material and demand detailed analysis. They also require you to read between the lines and engage in detective work.
- ► Book reviews focus intensely on your own individual response to what you read, nurturing independent thought.
- ► Other sorts of class exercises and assignments can make for variety and stimulate interest, but should not trespass unduly on the time required for private study.

There is more to studying history than writing essays, and in this chapter we shall look at the most important other types of exercise likely to be met. Particularly worth discussion here are the examinations which are set, usually at the end of a course, to test achievement and contribute, partly or wholly, to the final mark. The merits of examinations are often debated, and it is important to understand their real significance in the process of learning – methods and interpretations as well as facts. Further, a type of exercise hugely important in the discipline of history is the *document criticism exercise*, which requires the student to focus narrowly on the appraisal of a specific piece of documentary text; we shall look at an example of such an exercise to demonstrate what can be learned from it. Briefer comments on other sorts of assignments and classroom exercises will follow.

Examination answers

Examinations are of different sorts. Sometimes the questions are revealed in advance, sometimes unknown until the question paper is sighted in the examination room; sometimes it is permitted to bring in notes and printed material, sometimes not. Sometimes 'take-home' examination questions are given out, for the students to answer at leisure in the following few days, with ample opportunity to consult sources.

Historical study requires considerable reading and thought about the interpretation of evidence and the solution of problems arising from conflicting or ambiguous evidence. It is difficult to hold in the mind all the results of this work, or to draw together the threads of study conducted during a long period and see the patterns of meaning in the whole picture. Revision for an examination serves the pedagogical purpose of requiring students to draw the threads together, to survey the whole field, to look at the big picture, thus helping them to fix in mind the issues and problems that are important in the study they have conducted. It is especially valuable in this way if the examination questions are not known in advance.

Mao Tse-tung (Mao Zedong) condemned examinations as ambushes staged by enemy forces, and there is no doubt that, in impoverished educational cultures where learning is done by rote and teaching is unimaginative, examinations can occasion mental anguish with little intellectual reward. However, where the focus is on the really interesting problems of getting to grips with issues of interpretation, the pain of revision can be compensated for by progress in historical illumination, the illumination which Penelope Lively compared to 'some sort of divine revelation'.

Progress in historical illumination is not achieved by the successful completion of a limited number of specific routine tasks; it comes from constant immersion in the context. From the point of view of the examiner, therefore, it is important to assess what students have learned by reading and thinking throughout the period of study.

An examination with questions unknown in advance has the purpose of affording some measure of students' success in engaging in historical reading and thinking about the whole of the subject examined, and it does so in a way that can, in principle, eliminate the bogey of plagiarism, intended or inadvertent.

Open book examinations: sometimes it is permitted to bring in notes and printed material, photocopies or even reference books. This can, in theory, have the merit of allowing students to focus on the intellectually important issues of interpretation rather than facts for their own sake, since the facts do not have to be memorized but can be checked on the spot. However, in practice it encourages students to treat the occasion as a test of their ability to exploit handy portable sources of information and to identify pieces of information on demand. This is a skill of a sort, useful in various scholarly disciplines (perhaps especially in law) and not without value in history; but it is inimical to the cultivation of independent thought about problems of interpretation, and it opens the door to plagiarism.

Closed book examinations: here the student writes answers to questions set, without being able to look anything up. Different types of question may be set. Here, it is only the essay-type question that goes to the heart of history-writing skill and is relevant to the concerns of this book but, for contrast, let us first notice two others:

- *Short answer questions:* these are essentially factual questions calling for a demonstration that real knowledge has been obtained about details of history. In a paragraph, it is possible to go a little way beyond mere memorization of facts learned by rote and to show awareness of the significance of the topics treated within the context of the problems that have been studied. A certain degree of historical understanding can be shown as well as factual knowledge.

- *Multiple choice questions:* these merely require the identification, within a small range of options, of the right answers to factual questions. For some types of learning this can have a useful function. For history, in the senior forms of schools and in universities, it has only marginal value, if any. It has nothing to do with the understanding of historical context, or with independent thought about problems of interpretation. Such tests do not provide useful assessments of qualities that really matter to the writing of history.

Here, therefore, we need to be concerned chiefly with essay-type examination questions. These are traditional in examinations. They are of the same type as are suitable for essays, testing students' ability to think independently about problems of interpretation where there is conflicting evidence. Students cannot be expected to quote primary sources as evidence (except for a few important phrases here and there), or to cite sources in footnotes, but they can be expected to display knowledge of the context and to argue coherently on the basis of what they know for their favoured solutions to problems.

Good advice on dealing with essay-type questions is much the same in history as in other humanities subjects, or indeed subjects of scholarship generally, where such points as these apply:

- Make sure that you have understood exactly what is meant by the question. Do not start making notes or writing until you know positively that you understand it, know how to deal with it, and can successfully write an answer to it.

- In history especially, it is to be expected that a question has been chosen not just to call forth your factual knowledge about some topic but because it elicits some particular problem of interpretation. However innocuous it seems, it carries with it some ambiguity or conflict of evidence about which there has been debate. Show that you understand what the underlying problem is.

- To avoid diffuseness, show early on in each answer, perhaps in the first sentence, that you understand what sort of answer is needed and what, in a nutshell, your answer is going to be. This is good examiner psychology; the examiner is anxious to find out quickly whether you really appreciate what is wanted and can come up with the right sort of answer.

- Show that you understand allusions. Names of people or places, technical terms, jargon and portmanteau phrases need to be explained in those cases where, if there were no explanation, it might be suspected that you were repeating material from books without knowing what it means.

- Questions may be worth the same number of points, or different numbers. Budget your time accordingly. Do not spend so much time on favourite questions that there is not enough left to deal adequately with others. Almost maximum points awarded for one superb answer will not compensate for failure on others. Rigorously allow adequate time for writing all answers.

Document criticism

In a document criticism exercise, you are given an extract from a document or primary source and asked to write a criticism of it – that is, an analysis of its contents, explaining whatever needs to be explained. Sometimes you may be told who wrote it and from what work it is taken; sometimes you may be expected to infer this as part of the exercise.

Document criticism is important because it clearly focuses attention on the raw material of history. As you confront a primary source, you are in the same position as the scholar engaging in research; you are looking at the past through a window which it opens upon itself, not through the lenses of some other modern observer's research.

What this experience offers, then, is an opportunity to play the detective on the same clues that the professional historians use – the records of the past which the past has left us. You are not tempted to paraphrase the work of other writers. You are thrown onto your own resources – it is up to you to make whatever sense you can of the material in front of you.

A document criticism exercise is quite different from an essay. Do not treat the given documentary extract simply as a cue to show all you know about the subject of it in general. The extract is the actual material that you must closely investigate, point by point.

The 'criticism' you are expected to practise in a document criticism exercise is in the sense of critical appraisal – not just accepting things as given but examining them from all aspects to see what clues they give. The document in front of you is an object of study, just as a microbe on a microscope slide, a chemical in a test tube, or a shard of ancient pottery is an object of study for people in other disciplines.

A useful exercise is to forget, for the time being, all the particular knowledge you have about the document and its context and try to look at it with fresh eyes, uninfluenced by things you have read about its context. Concentrate on the actual content, without projecting preconceived ideas on it. If this were the only piece of evidence for the matters it describes, what would it show? What questions does it raise? This will compel you to focus on the evidence of what is there in the document.

Having identified the ideas and questions which arise from this perspective, you can then apply to them all your background knowledge derived from other reading, in order to discuss just what this document shows or suggests about the past which it reflects. Keep the focus on the document itself. Your use of other sources should not have the effect of turning your discussion into an essay, citing evidence from a variety of sources. You will probably not be expected to supply any footnotes, unless to pages of the document itself.

In applying your knowledge of the background, you will be seeking to explain as far as possible the author's identity and purpose, the situation in which the work was written, the intended audience, the historical significance of the matters treated in the extract, its value and reliability as source material, and the meaning of all the allusions made – names, technical terms, specific incidents or institutions and so on.

You can move back and forth between internal and external evidence (things said in the text and things you know about the context), commenting on different aspects in whatever order is indicated by the logic of your discussion.

A sample document criticism exercise

Here is an extract from a sixteenth-century Indian account of the life of the ruler Akbar the Great, written by the courtier Abu'l Fazl. If you were given the extract as a study assignment, you might or might not be given this information. If not, identifying the source would be part of the exercise. It is essentially a piece of detective work.

> One of the occurrences was the testing of the silent of speech. There was a great meeting, and every kind of enlightenment was discussed. In the 24th Divine year, H.M. said that speech came to every tribe from hearing, and that each remembered from another from the beginning of existence. If they arranged that human speech did not reach them, they certainly would not have the power of speech. If the fountain of speech bubbled over in one of them, he would regard this as Divine speech, and accept it as such. As some who heard this appeared to deny it, he, in order to convince them, had a *serai* built in a place which civilized sounds did not reach. The newly born were put into that place of experience, and honest and active guards were put over them. For a time tongue-tied wetnurses were admitted there. As they had closed the door of speech, the place was commonly called the Gang Mahal (the dumb-house). On the 29th (Amardad – 9th August 1582) he went out to hunt. That night he stayed in Faizabad, and next day he went with a few special attendants to the house of experiment. No cry came from that house of silence, nor was any speech heard there. In spite of their four years they had no part of the talisman of speech, and nothing came out except the noise of the dumb. What the wise Sovereign had understood several years before was on this day impressed on the hearts of the formalists and the superficial. This became a source of instruction to crowds of men. H.M. said, 'Though my words were proved, they still are saying the same things with a tongueless tongue. The world is a miserable abode of sceptics. To shut the lips is really to indulge in garrulity. They have hamstrung the camel of the Why and Wherefore, and have closed the gate of speech with iron walls.'[1]

A sample criticism follows. Notice that it is not just concerned to show what is wrong with the document. There are many more interesting things to discover than whether the author is biased and whether he can be trusted to tell the truth. Anything that can be explained is worth explaining, and anything that is mentioned may have a significance worth seeking.

> This passage comes from the *Akbarnāma*, an account of the antecedents and history of the emperor Akbar the Great (r. 1556–1605), by his friend and courtier Abu'l Fazl (1551–1602). The ruler referred to as H.M is Akbar himself, and the passage describes an experiment Akbar made to find whether human beings have the faculty of speech given to them as a divine gift (as orthodox Muslim teachers at the court argued), or whether they have to learn speech from others.

The meeting referred to, at which 'every kind of enlightenment was discussed', was one of Akbar's famous colloquies, at which he would invite representatives of known religions to discuss doctrines in his presence. Here, the opinions of the influential Muslim teachers at court, with their claims to authority, were freely exposed to discussion with proponents of the liberal mystic sects which they regarded as heterodox, or of Hinduism, or even of Christianity. Abu'l Fazl was a keen opponent of the faction of court teachers; Akbar was very liberal in his religious views and therefore inclined to support Abu'l Fazl.

The Divine year mentioned identifies the era used by Abu'l Fazl, beginning with Akbar's accession. His ready use of this era conforms to his attitude of reverence towards the emperor, an attitude which pervades the whole work – Akbar is always represented as right and always portrayed as wise, even supernaturally so. We need to remember that Akbar's patronage meant everything to the author, who was able to prosper as court favourite and high official in the face of the hostile faction of orthodox Muslim teachers only by the grace of his royal patron.

Akbar is described here as displaying his august wisdom by conducting an intriguingly scientific-looking experiment to see whether speech is a gift of God, in order to give evidence in refutation of the doctrine of the orthodox faction. Abu'l Fazl would have been eager to celebrate the success of an experiment with this purpose. In an exercise of royal power which today looks arbitrary and callous, the ruler had new-born infants isolated from all the sounds of speech for a number of years. They were placed in a *serai*, ordinarily a rest-house for travellers but here probably just a walled compound. Four years later, Akbar's scepticism about the Muslim teachers' dogma was vindicated by discovering that, lacking human intermediaries, God had not given speech to the infants, to the dismay of the 'formalists and the superficial', the Muslim teachers who claimed the authority of wisdom in the prescriptions of Muslim scripture.

Abu'l Fazl had a strong vested interest in the outcome of the experiment which he describes, for, as he represents it, it was a blow against the orthodox faction and a demonstration of the all-wise monarch's powers which owed nothing to institutionalized religion.

But can we trust the author? Interestingly, this is one episode for which we have a cross-reference in a totally different sort of source, a report by a Jesuit missionary who met Akbar. As the modern translator notes, Father Jerome Xavier understood that Akbar conducted the experiment in order to see whether, by-passing the human speech of the society into which the infants were born, a supernatural Divine Tongue would be given to them directly. On this account, Akbar was much less sceptical about speech as a divine gift than the *Akbarnāma* suggests.

This, if true, puts the matter in another light, and encourages us to see Akbar as not only callous but also credulous. Both these judgments, though, are inappropriate to the age in which Akbar lived – he was less cruel than other kings (especially his successor Jahangir), and more open-minded than most.

The words attributed to Akbar at the end of the extract were probably not actually uttered by him just as reported; they were Abu'l Fazl's gloss on the episode. They were probably approved by the ruler once written, though, for the author went to his patron frequently while writing the work for authoritative editorial decisions, and indeed the *Akbarnāma* was written first and foremost for Akbar to hear (not to read – he was illiterate).

The quotation of Akbar's words at the end of the extract is cryptic. It probably indicates that the members of the orthodox faction were not convinced by the experiment as they should have been, and that they persisted with their irrational adherence to dogmas.

What we see from this passage is literature in the service of an idea – the idea of Akbar's government as a new sort of power in India, entitled to rule over all men, Muslim and Hindu, because of the ruler's divine wisdom that was independent of pre-existing religious institutions. This was the programme which offered to people like Abu'l Fazl their only guarantee of security and recognition.

Book reviews

Another sort of exercise which might be assigned is a book review. You are asked to read a particular book and write a review of it within a given word limit.

What is important here is to write down *your own independent and individual response* to reading the book. You are not expected to become an expert on the subject matter and criticize the work in the way that a scholarly reviewer would. You are expected to show what you, with your particular background knowledge, have got out of reading the book. Nobody can tell you *how* you should respond. Just read the book thoughtfully and enquiringly, and see what happens in your mind as you do so. Then sum this up in writing.

As you can see, one intended benefit of this exercise is the same as in the case of a document criticism – it is designed to encourage independent thought in a direct confrontation with some source material. You are expected to say what you think of what you read, not what somebody else has written about it. The teacher wants to be able to hear your voice in the words of the review, not an imperfect recollection of the voices of other people.

Here are some of the questions you can ask yourself about what you read in order to map out your thoughts about it:

- What sort of book is it – a textbook, a book for the general reader, a research-based monograph, or what?
- For what sort of audience does the author seem to be writing? Some books are addressed to the small number of specialists who can criticize every sentence. Others seek to make their text appealing and comprehensible to almost anybody.
- When was it written? The date of the first edition may tell you much. The same things cannot be expected from a new book addressing recent findings and a book originally written long ago.
- What was the author's background? Where did he stand on the big issues of controversy? This is not strictly relevant to any judgment of the *merits* of a book, but knowing the answers can help you understand the author's assumptions and purposes.
- Why was the book written? This is always worth thought. What was the gap in the literature on the subject that the author wanted to fill? Was there a prevailing conventional belief about the subject that he wanted to challenge?
- How successfully did the writer fill the gap? You may not know enough about the rest of the literature to answer this question confidently. It is worth thinking about all the same – you may pick up useful clues from the introduction and the conclusion.
- Is there plenty of properly documented evidence? The answer may be suggested by the density of footnotes, but you need to look carefully at the way the sources are handled. Check whether the arguments offered depend at any points on undocumented evidence.
- Is it well argued? Even without knowing anything about the subject beforehand, you can decide how well it is argued by examining the way in which the evidence (assuming it is sound) is used.
- Is the language tendentious? Is the argument presented fairly, with proper attention to different perspectives?
- Is it clearly expressed and readable?
- Has care been taken with the critical apparatus? It should have a good index and either a thorough annotated bibliography or a review of the scholarly literature in an early chapter, discussing its treatment of the issues in which the author is interested. Other points are the explanation of abbreviations, especially for primary sources, the consistent identification of sources, the use of illustrations, tables, graphs and other matter, and the table of contents as a guide to the plan of attack.

One approach to writing a review may be useful but must be followed with caution: look for reviews of the same book in the journals. Of course, it would thwart the essential purpose of the exercise if you were to write your review as if it were an essay based on the other reviews. The whole point is that you should come up with thoughts of your own about what you have read. You may, however, be able to stimulate those thoughts, and find out some good relevant facts worth pondering, by looking at other reviews.

To find these other reviews, you will need to identify the right journals and the right years. The right journals are the ones devoted to the same field of study as the book you are looking at. The right year will probably not be the year of first publication of the book. An academic book may remain in print for years before learned journals start producing reviews of it. You therefore have to guess which volume to examine first. Start with the volume of any journal that is dated two years later than the book's publication, then work back and forward from there.

Seminar introduction papers

A student may be asked to introduce discussion of a topic studied in a particular week by speaking for some minutes about the topic. The purpose of this may be to raise good questions for seminar discussion; submission of a written paper to go with, or follow, this oral presentation may be required as an assignment. In such a case, the written assignment is not performing the same function as an essay, which is supposed to be the writer's best attempt to solve a particular problem by using the best available sources. Its function, rather, is to review the issues that need to be confronted in discussion of a topic. It may comment briefly on the primary sources available, show why certain problems in the interpretation of them arise, identify the main ideas advanced by scholars who have written about the topic, set out the points of agreement and disagreement between them, and point to the most interesting issues that must be tackled in coming to any conclusion about the merits of different interpretations.

A paper of this sort may be required in advance for copying and distributing, or for assessment as an independent discussion written before the student can appropriate ideas raised during the seminar discussion itself. Alternatively, it may be required later, so that ideas raised in the seminar discussion may be included, and so that it may be fashioned into a more polished treatment of the subject. There may or may not be a requirement for documentation and bibliography to follow the same rules as apply to essays. On the whole it is probably better if these rules are applied.

Reports

Some assignments might involve writing a report – for example, a summary of things read in a certain period or for a certain purpose. This can be a useful short-term revision tool, helping to restore to memory what you have read and to organize knowledge into patterns, aiding understanding. It also requires careful reflective reading and skill in summarizing succinctly, thus serving some of the same purposes as comprehension exercises and précis. A report, however, is quite different from an essay.

Some other varieties of class assignment

Nowadays various sorts of exercise are often set in order to stimulate reading, independent thought and collaborative study. Some of these are influenced by practices often adopted in schools, and may seem more suited to the school classroom; but participating in them can sometimes turn out to be genuinely rewarding (although organized activities should always be in an appropriate balance with private study, which requires plenty of time). Here are some examples:

- *A journal or diary of historical study.* This would typically be conducted over a period, recording the sources read and offering thoughts about what sources were particularly interesting to read and why, what sorts of questions arose in your mind from your reading, and how well the study plan worked. This record may be written online as a blog, open to comment by fellow students.

- *An online posting to be read and discussed by fellow students,* as a single specific task. It could involve anything relevant to the shared historical study and deemed worth sharing with fellow students for discussion.

- *An interactive online exercise in the reinforcement of routine techniques,* assessed automatically. Such tests could include, for example, exercises in correct documentation format; the design could automatically provide explanations and further questions when answers are wrong. Teachers could monitor the resulting scores and identify students' success in mastering the techniques involved. (Such tests are best applied to techniques rather than factual historical knowledge; in the latter case they may incur the disadvantages of multiple choice examination questions.)

- *A 'historical orienteering' exercise.* Such assignments are described in Chapter 3 (pp. 26–7).

- *Re-enactment of a specific historical event or encounter*, with impromptu dialogue to stimulate historical imagination and explore the points of view of the individuals represented.
- *Team competition in the staging of scripted productions*. These would be documentaries exploring chosen historical episodes or problems. The contents might include dramatic re-enactment, miniature lectures, dialogue, and the showing of slides or recordings.
- *A formal debate on a historical problem*, with a motion to be voted on and speeches by those proposing, opposing and seconding.

Questions

1   What sort of examination format do you think is most appropriate for a typical course of study in history? Why?

2   In this chapter, several types of test or assignment are listed which can contribute to the consolidation or enrichment of a student's learning. Which of them seems to be most specifically useful for study in the discipline of history? Why?

From Essay to Thesis

Chapter overview

► A student history essay fosters many of the same methods and skills as more advanced work, from an undergraduate thesis to a PhD thesis.

► Both essay and thesis should use the best available sources, but for a postgraduate thesis they will be the best sources existing anywhere, in any language.

► At the higher levels, the supervisor offers guidance and suggests sources, but only so as to help the student find and interpret fresh sources independently.

► The research student must read extensively, until he knows as much about his topic as the authors he reads.

► His thesis may not take shape until the 'light-bulb' moment, when he first detects a problem which others have not solved and which he may be able to solve.

► A major thesis cannot be planned and written in one go; it must take shape gradually through the experimental writing of sections.

► Thesis preparation requires the writing of a literary review, which will help the writer to analyse the current state of knowledge and the holes in it which demand to be plugged.

► A historical thesis must contribute to the sum of scholarly knowledge. This should take the form of rigorous analysis of sources leading to heightened understanding of one part of the past, not necessarily a new theory about how the past in general works.

A standard undergraduate history essay is at one end of a scale. At the other end is the full-blown PhD thesis. In the course of your studies, you may move step-by-step up the scale, being asked to write progressively longer and more scholarly essays. How do these later progressions compare with the ordinary undergraduate essay which begins the series? What really makes them different? At each advance, what new set of techniques or facts needs to be learned?

On the whole, it is fair to say that the standard undergraduate essay is a baby version of the sort of thesis you may eventually write, and it is designed to develop many of the same qualities as those displayed by a postgraduate thesis. As you move up the scale, the essays you write will continue to call for the same techniques that have figured in earlier chapters of this book. Of course, there are certain particular differences, and this chapter is designed in large part to give some understanding of those differences. This may help you to understand what is expected at each stage along the way.

The ladder from essay to thesis

Minor essays or term papers figure as standard exercises in undergraduate study. In some cases, versions of these requiring more independent research may be called 'long essays'.

In later years you may be required to write an even longer sort of essay which will be called an 'undergraduate thesis'. Honours students may spend a substantial part of one year writing honours theses which are supposed to display a great deal of independent research. Exceptionally, these may be scholarly enough to be considered worth publishing in some format, perhaps as departmental papers.

MA courses by teaching and research include minor theses; these may sometimes exploit primary sources well enough to warrant publication.

Finally, full-time research for master's and doctoral degrees is supposed to yield theses that are original contributions to scholarship and can possibly be published by academic publishers.

In the earlier stages of advance from undergraduate essay to postgraduate thesis, the new approaches required are for the most part qualitatively not very different from the techniques already discussed in earlier chapters. What is needed is more detail, more thorough reading, more chasing up of elusive facts. Gradually and cumulatively, there is an advance to what becomes eventually a new perspective. The nature of the gradual change is therefore best understood by looking ahead to see what happens in its later stages, in work on a postgraduate thesis, and in the following sections there will be frequent reference to the experience of those working on doctoral dissertations.

The principle of best available sources

Your student history essay is supposed to be about history, be academic, be an essay, and count as literature. So is a PhD thesis. Your essay is an apprentice exercise leading you towards the increasingly sophisticated exercises further up the ladder.

So what essentially makes the difference between the two ends of the ladder? One of the best ways of making the distinction is provided by the principle of best available sources, already noticed here. A student is expected to look at primary sources, even if only in the form of edited extracts published in collections with introductions designed for the student. Where time and prior experience are limited, this may be the best that can be expected.

Much the same applies to secondary sources: the student will not have the opportunity to read all the conceivably relevant articles or other publications that exist.

With experience, however, the student can draw closer and closer to real scholarship by becoming able to exploit better and better ranges of sources. Eventually, it becomes possible to burrow into catalogues and find many good primary sources, even unpublished ones.

Major advances are made when you can move out from your own institution's library to others in the same town, or further afield, and ultimately you will conduct *fieldwork* wherever in the world you can consult the best existing sources in archives, museums and libraries.

A parallel major advance is made when you take the time to learn whatever languages are necessary to understand the best sources, primary or secondary.

For real scholarship, is it essential to learn foreign languages?

Clearly, this question does not apply when all the sources likely to be useful for your research topic are in English. In other cases, the shortest answer is yes. For scholarly research, it is necessary to read the best known available sources, and if these are in any language other than (for our purposes) English, then you need a passable reading knowledge of such language or languages.

However, this answer must be qualified; there are legitimate exceptions. It all depends what exactly your research topic is.

There are topics that enable the researcher to concentrate on sources from countries where various languages are spoken, and yet to produce valuable interpretations without moving outside English. Topics in economic, diplomatic, administrative, military and imperial history are the most obvious sorts. For example, the archives of colonial powers in Asia and other parts of the world are rich in material for detailed studies of colonial administration and for diplomatic relations, and the historian of the British empire, or the French, or the Dutch, cannot be expected to roam freely through the literatures produced in local languages all round the world.

Ideally, of course, a good understanding of local society through the eyes of local people might always give the historian a better perspective. However, many good books have been written without it.

The difference between thesis supervisors and teachers

As you advance further in your studies, and the essays you write are based on more and more detailed research, you will increasingly be expected to consult the best sources available anywhere to answer questions that have not previously been decisively answered. This progression marks a real break from the experience of study at lower levels; it is a sort of weaning process, an initiation.

When your essay turns into a thesis, and your teacher becomes a supervisor, you are no longer an apprentice being taught by masters. After completing a postgraduate thesis, it is to be hoped that you will have qualified as a teacher of others (*doctor* means 'teacher'). The work of writing the thesis should be powerfully active in fostering real intellectual independence. You are not going to write a compilation of others' opinions. You are going to compel your readers to share your own independently formed opinions.

During much of your undergraduate study, you were reading sources set for study by teachers familiar with the contents of them and well able to raise good questions about them. Now, you are reading sources with which the supervisor is not necessarily very familiar, and you are supposed to go on and discover by yourself a lot more sources which have not previously been looked at together with the questions in mind which you hope to ask. You are expected, by your own efforts, to struggle *to the boundaries of current knowledge*. In your earlier studies, you were receiving instruction from others, carrying out specific tasks that they set you. Now, by contrast, although you are receiving guidance from your supervisor, it is all designed to help you propel yourself into territory where you will know best what paths to follow, what means of progress to adopt. You must get used to taking initiatives. Doctoral candidates can hope eventually to know more than anyone else in the world at least about some aspects of their topic.

Reading, reading and more reading

This ambition to lead the world may seem impossibly daunting, but in fact, so long as good solid foundations have been laid by your undergraduate study, it should be quite possible, and more of an adventure than a trial. (Sadly, it occasionally happens that a postgraduate is accepted for a research programme without a good enough grounding in specific relevant undergraduate studies; when this happens, the situation should be terminated immediately.)

It is common experience for thesis students to spend many months at the beginning floundering about, experimenting with successive projects without understanding where they will lead, mapping out unrealistic goals, and reading things that seem to be no help whatsoever. Much of the first year may later appear to have been wasted.

This need not happen, however, so long as you do plenty of reading, all of which is in the general field of your emerging thesis topic, and so long as the things you read are all connected to one another in some way. If you do not at all understand the relevance or meaning of any source, drop it completely; it may make sense to you later on. Read as much as you can from any and all sources – primary, secondary and even tertiary if it seems interesting and good.

Journals are particularly good to read. Work through long runs of back numbers, scanning and skimming to see what might be relevant and interesting. Allow yourself to be distracted by other topics; the very fact that they look interesting may indicate that they have some theoretical significance, some point of comparison about them which will help you to refine your thought about your own topic later.

Find out from reviews, review articles and correspondence in journals what are the issues of debate among scholars in the field, what they like and dislike about each other's work.

By the same token, browsing in the most relevant h-net network or networks will help you to recognize yourself as potentially a member of a community, interested in attending debates, going to lectures, reviewing books and going to conferences.

All this will gradually lay the basis on which you will be thinking increasingly historically, gradually building up a pattern of remembered ideas about the past and connections among past events.

The light-bulb moment

At first you will not have a very clear idea of what precisely will be new about your thesis; after all, it will have to be new to you too at first.

Do not mistakenly think that you can hammer it out right at the beginning by writing a plan for a fixed list of chapters; such a list may, at some stages, be helpful in stimulating thought, but only if it is infinitely provisional, flexible and temporary. That is, it will be provisional only until the point when you really know what you are doing and start mapping out the details of your actual thesis in earnest.

For this to happen, you first need by constant reading to develop a feel for the contours of scholarship in your field.

You will keep noticing certain ideas cropping up in many writers' work, and certain topics which historians have found problematic and difficult. You will find yourself agreeing with some and disagreeing with others, and you will become aware of issues about which nobody seems to have any better ideas than you have. Some topics may seem never to have been dealt with properly.

That is when a light may go on in your head, shining on the ghostly image of a possible thesis, an idea of your own which you can explore further and develop. This may be the moment when your real thesis is conceived.

If your further work shows that what you want to do is at least a bit different from what anybody else has done, and you think you can find adequate evidence to support it, then your thesis may come to birth.

Writing

The writing that you do in the course of your study will be largely determined by your supervisor. In certain stages, it may well consist of drafting one chapter (or section of a chapter) each week, to be read out and discussed.

As noted above, however, it will probably not be realistic to expect to map out in the earlier stages the actual succession of chapters that will finally appear in the thesis. The important principle to understand is that you will not know what you want to say until you write it down, and you will not be able to write it down until you know what you want to say. (This dilemma is why so many writers suffer from 'writer's block'.) What this means in practice is that you will advance, not by creating in your mind a plan for the entire thesis and then writing it out, but by writing many drafts of potential bits of the thesis, abandoning many and stitching others together as your ideas about what the thesis will say, and the relevance of the bits you have written, become clearer.

So, whenever you have read enough about any specific subtopic within the field to suggest that you may have something to say which could go into the thesis, it is good to make a miniature essay of it on your own initiative immediately. The act of writing this miniature essay will help you enormously to clarify the evidence that has been assembled and its possible significance for the thesis. It is much easier to focus on making one brick than to design the whole house.

The literature review

As part of your work on your thesis, you may be formally required to write a literature review. Even if not, it is nevertheless necessary to produce one. It needs to grow as you work on sources, displaying a record of your progress. At some early stage, you may be required to present it to your supervisor and perhaps to a seminar. When your thesis is complete, a final revised version of it will figure as perhaps an early chapter, or as a substantial part of the introduction.

The literature review, quite unlike a review of a book, is a discussion of all the important sources available for the study of your topic. Up to a point, it is a little like an extended annotated bibliography. It identifies a substantial number of sources, primary and secondary, and comments on their usefulness for the research.

However, it goes further than a bibliography, and it has a different purpose. A bibliography attached to a book is a guide to reading on the subject of the book, or to research sources for the interested reader. A bibliography attached to a student essay is a record of sources used in work on the essay. A literature review, on the other hand, is constructed in the first place as a tool for the purpose of prosecuting research; the author is himself the main intended reader. The systematic description of available sources, identifying the nature of their content and their relevance to the research topic, is a necessary early part of the research itself; it contributes directly to the conceptualization of the central problems to be addressed, indicating what questions have been answered satisfactorily by others and what questions remain.

This sort of review, in its final form within the thesis, functions to show the reader what the dissertation can hope to achieve by setting out clearly what problems have already been identified, what solutions have been advanced, how satisfactory the writer believes these solutions to be, what are the problems worth tackling, and how, given the nature of the sources available, these problems can best be approached.

In order to achieve these aims, a literature review must be much more than a list of sources with comments. It must be arranged in such a way as to show what are the problems, what the dissertation need not attempt because certain things have been done by others, what it cannot attempt because the sources do not exist to make it possible, and what it may usefully attempt because the means are at hand. The accounts given of particular sources need to take their place within an overarching discussion of the topic in general.

What constitutes real scholarship?

A thesis, unlike an undergraduate essay, is supposed to demonstrate real scholarship, or else the examiners will not accept it. What is this real scholarship? In fact, the ingredients of essay writing recommended in this book all contribute to the nurturing of the skills that ripen in the thesis. The difference between a beginner's essay and a good PhD thesis may be big, but in essence it is simply identified by listing qualities already discussed here. The list might look something like this:

- The thesis uses all the best sources available to anybody, not just a selection.
- These sources have been appraised with well-informed reference to their context.
- Their significance for the writer's conclusions is clearly spelled out, with all the relevant evidence properly displayed and fairly assessed.
- The conclusions are set out coherently, and are shown to be consistent with the evidence.
- The best possible arguments *against* these conclusions are given sufficient attention.
- The thesis as a whole constitutes a useful addition to knowledge.

The first and last items here are the only ones that seem to mark a clear and decisive difference from student essays. The first has been discussed; the last may raise further questions.

Your thesis can be considered to be a useful addition to knowledge if it draws good conclusions by interrogating new sources not previously examined, or if it interrogates sources already known but asks new questions which lead to good conclusions; that is, conclusions which are reached by good historical methods using the sources rigorously, and which are likely to be interesting to historians because they suggest new ideas or open up promising new questions.

Sometimes, historians who are influenced by methods current in scientific disciplines will claim that a thesis must add to knowledge by offering some new theoretical insight. That is, it must shed light not just on its own particular slice of the past, but on theories about the past in general. This implies that what it suggests about human behaviour in one place and time might then be generalized to predict what will be discovered from other contexts with appropriate characteristics.

However, this is probably setting the bar too high. A thesis offering a sufficiently rigorous account of some piece of local history, using sources that have not been used for such a purpose before, can add to knowledge about localities if it does a good job in the ways discussed above. Human society is not a laboratory in which the historian expects to discover new laws. Sometimes, the best is the enemy of the good; we must not demand impossible precision or certainty. History seeks evidence from the context of the events studied, and context can be expanded indefinitely to take in more facts which might be relevant. Complete certainty about the correctness of a theory cannot be achieved, but increasing familiarity with the past certainly can be.

This sort of familiarity is achieved by good method and thoroughness in studying the sources, with a mind constantly alert for new perspectives and clues, rather than by applying general theories about the nature of history. Good advice about writing theses is the same as about writing undergraduate essays.[1] So, to equip yourself to undertake more advanced undergraduate work, you need to apply two principles:

1 Continue to cultivate the techniques described in all earlier chapters, but in more detail and taking more time over each operation.
2 However modestly, work towards the ideal of the postgraduate thesis, which uses the best sources available anywhere in the world and makes a contribution to the total of human knowledge.

Questions

1 Reread the quotation from Penelope Lively at the beginning of Chapter 1. Does her reference to 'debate and conflicting evidence' seem to you to go to the heart of the nature of historical research? If so, or if not, explain.

2 To what extent does history seem to you to belong among the arts, and to what extent among the sciences?

Appendix: A Note on Historiography

To study history is also to study the writing of history, or 'historiography'. Students are commonly expected to study major works by historians, not only to learn about the subjects treated by these works, but also to learn from them about the methods, varieties and, indeed, the history of history. In theory at least, if you are to understand history well, it is desirable to know something about the range of different histories – different ages and parts of the world, different ideas and ideologies informing the historian's purposes, and different tools used to fulfil those purposes.

If you explore the literature by historians on history writing, you are bound to be struck by the amount of disagreement. Every writer is naturally anxious to explain and justify his own favoured ideas about what is important in the study of the past, trying to make sure that no reader will be misled by the folly of other writers with different ideas. Some books are occasionally cantankerous; this is only to be expected at times from people devoted to the service of Clio, the muse of history – proud of their service, they are assiduous in defence of what they see as good practice in that service. Many books, sometimes the same ones, are fired by their authors' enthusiasm for history and are paradigms of eloquence and lucidity. But from such books, whatever the styles and attitudes that shape them, much may be learned.

Your essay writing can benefit from some understanding of the historiographical background; if you know where an author belongs in the range of ideas and methods, what sorts of theories he regards as good and as bad, you can better understand what he is trying to do, and respond accordingly. What follows here is the merest sketch of the field. All that can be offered is a few examples of types and styles of history, and a few examples of historians who have written about their craft.

The history of history

When did academic history writing begin? We could start with ancient Greek civilization; after all, Herodotus (fifth century BC) has been called the father of history. Yet modern historians are looking for something more than the often implausible stories that he relates, something recognizable as the product of truly critical research.

You might think that, if an author tells you that he has examined all the sources assiduously and taken pains to get at the truth, his account of what has happened in the past must count as history. Think again; Thucydides (also fifth century BC) did this, and has, on that account, often been regarded as a genuine scientific historian, but more recent research suggests that his accounts of events were substantially moulded by aesthetic and literary principles. In India, the courtier Abu'l Fazl (16th century AD) did this too in his *Akbarnāma*; he may have been sincere, but his devotion to his imperial master Akbar was what really shaped his narrative. What historians are looking for as they chart their own discipline is the development of a set of standards actually applied to the critical sifting of evidence.

Even Edward Gibbon (1737–94), author of *The Decline and Fall of the Roman Empire*, a magnificent literary achievement, generally fails the test, and well into the nineteenth century eminent writers of histories such as Thomas Babington Macaulay (1800–59), who produced a magisterial *The History of England from the Accession of James the Second,* are commonly judged literary figures rather than fully academic historians in the modern sense.

Modern judgments generally converge on Barthold Georg Niebuhr (1776–1831) and Leopold Ranke (1795–1886) as founders of the academic historical tradition. Niebuhr, who taught at Bonn University, wrote among other things a history of Rome which in some ways laid the basis for the methods of critical research, based on detailed attention to primary sources. Ranke, who taught at the University of Berlin, did much to establish history as a distinct academic discipline that reflected on its methods, emphasizing the importance of an objective account of the past 'as it really was'; this required immersion in contemporary sources, deep familiarity with the languages in which they were written, and avoidance of the temptation to project modern ideas on the past.

On this foundation, the practice of historical research developed through the nineteenth century. Jacob Burckhardt (1818–97), a Swiss scholar who was a pupil of Ranke, evinced a concern with the cultural interpretation of history. His *The Civilization of the Renaissance in Italy* sought to present a portrait of the spirit of an age, seeing in the culture of the Renaissance a decisive turn to individualism in contrast to the corporate spirit of the Middle Ages. This sort of generalization nowadays looks somewhat glib, but his erudition and deep concern with understanding the cultural environment of a past age give his work lasting influence. Another major scholar was Theodor Mommsen (1817–1903), who taught law in

German and Swiss universities and wrote the monumental *The History of Rome*; his achievement was to reconstruct an ancient society from the painstaking and detailed study of a variety of primary sources, coins and inscriptions as well as texts. His scholarly editions of bodies of source material have attracted from modern experts in his field as much admiration as has his interpretative history. In 1902 he received the Nobel Prize for literature.

History writing in the nineteenth century concentrated especially on the actions of major political figures such as rulers, and on states and political institutions. The relative youth of the academic discipline, and the nature of the sources that presented themselves as the raw material for study (which often came from court archives or texts written by people close to centres of political power), perhaps predisposed to this orientation, but in the twentieth century it began to look incomplete; there has since been a reaction against what is regarded as schoolroom 'kings and battles' history. More recently, scholars have preferred to look for the important factors of historical changes in underlying social trends over long periods, rather than in the decisions of powerful individuals or the fortunes of national states. A widespread preoccupation among scholars has been with the social environment, closely analysing from local sources the pattern of life in the village, the market town, or the city street, seeking to understand behaviour and relationships within society as a whole.

This characterization applies exactly to the work of Marc Bloch (1886–1944), who taught in Strasbourg and later at the Sorbonne, Paris. He was an authority on medieval French history, applying to his research a keen interest in economic factors as they affect the life of society. He combined attention to local detail with a vision of broad horizons, understanding the present in relation to the past as well as vice versa, and exploring lines of influence that extended over time, often jumping across generations. His reflections on the techniques of his discipline (in *The Historian's Craft,* an unfinished work cut short by his execution during the occupation) applied common sense in detail to the problems of unveiling the significance of sources. His principles helped to give form to the school of historical scholarship that grew in part from his work; so did his collaboration with Febvre in founding the journal *Annales,* a forum for historical work in the same tradition.

Lucien Febvre (1878–1956), although older than Bloch, survived him after the war and continued to run the *Annales,* contributing to the promotion of history writing that emphasized economic factors, society as a whole, and a broad vision of the larger context in space and time. This style shaped what is now known as the Annales School of history, which has influenced many scholars, although these have often established their own individual styles – for example Emmanuel Le Roy Ladurie (1929–), whose *The Peasants of Languedoc* is a vivid portrait of a single locality over a long period, exploring people's lives in intense detail.

A hugely influential figure in this tradition is Fernand Braudel (1902–85), who was much influenced by Lucien Febvre and carried to an extreme degree the Annales School's combination of local economic detail with broad vision and wide context. His best-known work, on the Mediterranean region (*La Méditerranée et le monde méditerranéen à l'époque de Philippe II*), applied an elaborate apparatus of economic and geographical analysis to the lives of people living in the region throughout history, identifying three levels of analysis: the familiar scale of historical events important to the explanation of things happening in the present; the underlying conjunction of conditions, particularly economic and environmental conditions, which shaped the longer term pattern of critical changes, and the deep slow rhythms of change that can be charted only over centuries and in a global context – the *longue durée*.

In the twentieth century, the nature and methods of historical study came to be more and more explicit, with many practitioners writing about the nature of their craft. Bloch's work, already mentioned, is an important example. In Britain, many historians looked critically at their discipline, and particularly at the political attitudes which often underlie a historian's view of the world. A thought-provoking contribution, which is still often cited, was made by Herbert Butterfield (1900–79), in his book *The Whig Interpretation of History* (1931). This has significance in calling attention to the way in which historians have commonly been tempted unthinkingly to judge the past about which they write as if it had to be seen as a stage in the onward march of progress towards a better future, culminating in our own present; this leads them to make villains of whoever did things that do not conform to today's values. Such judgments are often inappropriate. The 'Whig' party in earlier British history stood for liberal politics, the belief in progress, but the historians guilty of unthinking 'Whig' assumptions and anachronistic judgments could in their own politics be either liberal or conservative. Some have therefore criticized Butterfield's use of the term 'Whig'.

The belief in progress was strong. E.H. Carr (1892–1982) combined this belief with an acute consciousness of the potential deceptiveness of the sources used by the historian. In his *What is History?* (1961; based on a series of Cambridge lectures), he criticized the 'cult of facts' which treats them as totally objective realities; on the contrary, the selection and understanding of them, he argued, inevitably imposes on them the historian's interpretation: 'This element of interpretation enters into every fact of history.' Hence history is a sort of dialogue between present and past; historians cannot stand apart from their own society and judge the past absolutely. Ideas are shaped by conditions in the present society. Therefore the task of history is to seek heightened consciousness of these conditions. With progress and education come better possibilities for consciousness of the conditions that shape the present, and the historian can assist the enhancement of consciousness and thereby work against trends to mass manipulation.

Perhaps Carr was influenced by the conditions of the 1950s, which seemed to put progress, consciousness, reason and enlightened planning on the side of history. His views, though, went against the grain of the older tradition of writing history going back to Ranke, and some historians thought that he was mistaken in treating 'the cult of facts' so cavalierly, as if facts had no independent existence. For these historians, real historical scholarship requires submission to the discipline of meticulous attention to the primary sources. This more traditional point of view is well represented by the Tudor historian G.R. Elton (Sir Geoffrey; born G.R. Ehrenberg; 1921–94), who, in *The Practice of History* (1967), argued at length for the older values, emphasizing political and administrative factors of history and demanding that the historian should be, until his conclusions are formed, 'the servant of his evidence'. Elton holds up the work of Mommsen in editing documents as core historical scholarship, whereas Carr saw it as mere compilation.

Recent trends in the writing of history

In the latter part of the twentieth century, and down to our own times, historical scholarship has witnessed a proliferation of new trends and schools which could not be adequately charted even in a much bigger book than this. Many of these trends, seeking improved insights, have deliberately rejected aspects of traditional wisdom and tried out new subject matter and new methods. Some are major features of the contemporary intellectual landscape, yet here no more can be done than to point to them as varieties of, or influences on, history writing; they all deserve investigation if we are to acquire a proper sense of the ways in which history has changed.

Perhaps most conspicuous is Marxism itself. Marx was not a historian, but his view of history was at the core of his teaching, and for a period roughly corresponding to the third quarter of the twentieth century, Marxist or neo-Marxist thought was a major topic of study in various humanities departments of universities everywhere. Some Marxist historians became powerful influences, such as E.J. Hobsbawm (1917–2012), one of the foremost specialists in nineteenth-century social and economic history. The influence of Marxism on history was not confined to those who sought to apply, or even knew much about, Marxist theory as such; rather, with its emphasis on economic structures as underlying forces acting on motives and behaviour, it influenced the way people thought about historical explanation.

Social science, emphasizing quantitive methods, has been a major influence on the style of history writing rather than on a particular group or movement. The importance of economics, sociology, psychology and the other disciplines at the core of social science have made it inevitable that historians should increasingly attempt to incorporate more 'scientific' methods, particularly those involving the analysis of statistics, which has been boosted by information technology; historians can nowadays create graphs, maps, histograms and statistical breakdowns manipulating huge quantities of information. Richard Hofstadter (1916–70) has written about the considerable value for history which he attributes to the social sciences, while recognizing the important differences between the two types of study. On the other hand, even though one would expect the Annales School to identify itself with the social sciences, Braudel has objected that the latter cannot integrate the surface level of historical events with the fundamental, often geographical, conditions that shape the global and long-term trends of the *longue durée*. Theodore Zeldin (1933–) has argued that history has enjoyed a marriage with social sciences that is in some ways beneficial, but which risks smothering history's distinctive character; this character lies in its concern with the uniquely personal qualities of individuals in the past.

Postmodernism had an influence on humanities disciplines, including history, in the concluding decades of the twentieth century. It is not a specific theory but a cluster of movements, often centred on famous thinkers, which engage in criticism of conventional statements about almost anything. They are generally sceptical about claims that imply knowledge of the essential nature of objective realities which exist out there in the world, independently of our talking about them, and challenge conventional notions of what is central or fundamental to anything. This approach, applied to history, goes many steps further than E.H. Carr's distrust of claims to know facts with total objectivity. A prominent historian whose work exhibits postmodern attributes is Michel Foucault (1926–84), much of whose work dealt with the relation between power and knowledge; he argued that all history must be written in relation to concerns in the present. Postmodernist influences have inspired much interest in the relationship between historical and literary methods: if the sovereign reality of actual historical events 'as they actually were' is dethroned in favour of multiple points of view, is the story told by the historian more of a literary creation than a search for truth? Hayden White (1928–) has analysed in detail the problems raised by such perspectives.

A broad trend from the 1960s onward has been the rise of interest in writing 'people's history'. The nineteenth-century pioneers of historical methods were interested in places and periods (especially ancient Rome) for which the primary sources were, at first sight at least, not well able to illumine the history of ordinary people, but as more and more historians unearthed more and more sources, the writing of history 'from the bottom up' became an increasingly realistic project, especially for the history of recent generations. The Annales School paved the way; more recent historians have, however, been more interested in focusing on the disadvantaged underclasses as such, and one important development has been the emergence of 'subaltern history' in the domain of Indian history: the journal *Subaltern Studies* was started in India in 1981. The best-known historian in this movement is Ranajit Guha (1923–).

Gender history has become a conspicuous feature of the landscape, represented by a large number of prominent scholars. They are not concerned simply to write discussions of women into the historical record; their concern is also, and especially, to show how the relationships between the sexes are an important dimension of social articulation in all societies, contributing to the shaping of history and the worldviews adopted within cultures. Such concerns have been forcefully expressed by Joan Wallach Scott (1941–), who writes of gender as increasingly signifying 'the social organization of the relationship between the sexes' (1988). Many studies have been made with this perspective, leading to a re-envisioning of social history. Attention has also been given to the concept of 'masculinities' as a phenomenon of changing environments.

Recent years have seen a lot of historical writing about the lives of ordinary people, often experimenting with new sorts of sources; this trend has been conspicuous in Australia, where there has been a blossoming of critical self-consciousness about the fundamentals of history as a discipline. This is represented, for example, by Ann Curthoys (1945–) and John Docker (1945–), who steer a course between the extremes of literal-minded 'scientific' history and postmodern relativism to explore the nuances of technique where reflective historical interpretation can overlap the craftsmanship of literary narrative (*Is History Fiction?* 2005/2006/2010).

A different area of historical concern is the one generally labelled as public history. This has attracted much interest, particularly in the USA, although there has been considerable disagreement about how it should be defined. Public history can be broadly identified as the sort of historical work that goes on outside universities, notably as conducted by people involved in the preservation of cultural heritage, oral history, museology and the protection of historical environments. It is represented especially by projects concerned with buildings, cityscapes and the built environment, as well as by activities carried out within any sort of institution to make concrete local connections with the past. Australian historians have been active in this field, particularly in connection with the interaction between culture and urban environment.

This sort of concern is closely allied to the trend in mainstream historical scholarship to exploit many sorts of sources alongside written records. For example, Rhys Isaac (1937–2010), in his study of religious change in eighteenth-century Virginia (*The Transformation of Virginia, 1740–1790,* 1982), applied the techniques of the cultural anthropologist and examined closely the evidence of architecture, diet, costume and other features of culture in order to understand changes in people's behaviour; he was concerned specifically with reflections on the possibilities of new methods such as a combination of ethnographic and dramatic analysis (see particularly, in *The Transformation,* the section 'A discourse on the method: action, structure, and meaning', pp. 323–57). In *Car Wars: How the Car Won our Hearts and Conquered our Cities* (2004), Graeme Davison (1940–) examines the history of the car in later twentieth-century Australia not only to draw lessons about its symbolism and cultural significance in general but also, much more specifically, to explore its reflections of conflicts between the sexes, the generations, social and economic groups, the individual and the community, and the interests of health and safety versus those of speed and utility.

There is much more that could be said about this dynamic exploration of alternative sources that is in some ways transforming the practice of history, but it cannot be properly analysed here. This book has attempted to cast light on work within the core tradition of historical scholarship, which is founded on the critical appraisal of recorded words, and it is surely prudent to concentrate on this tradition if the introduction to the historian's craft is not to be confusing. But it is also fascinating to contemplate the rich promise of new insights to be won by future research as the methods of historical craftsmanship evolve.

These brief comments must suffice to indicate some of the range covered by the historical literature on history. Some references follow.

History writing and historical method: some references

Bentley, Michael, *Modern Historiography: An Introduction* (New York, Routledge), 1999.

Bloch, Marc, *The Historian's Craft,* trans. Peter Putnam (New York, Knopf), 1953.

Braudel, Fernand, 'History and the social sciences: the *longue durée*', in idem, *On History,* trans. Sarah Matthews (London, Weidenfeld & Nicolson), 1980, pp. 25–54.

——. *The Mediterranean and the Mediterranean World in the Age of Philip II*, trans. Sian Reynolds, 2 vols (New York, Harper & Row), 1972–4.

Burckhardt, Jacob, *The Civilization of the Renaissance in Italy* (New York, Dover Publications), 2010.

Butterfield, Herbert, *The Whig Interpretation of History* (London, G. Bell), 1931.

Cannon, John, ed., *The Historian at Work* (London, George Allen & Unwin), 1980.

Carr, Edward H., *What is History?*, ed. R.W. Davies (Harmondsworth, Penguin), 1990.

Curthoys, Ann and John Docker, *Is History Fiction?* (Sydney, University of New South Wales Press), 2005, 2006 rev. edn 2010.

Curthoys, Ann and Ann McGrath, eds, *Writing Histories: Imagination and Narration* (Melbourne, Monash Publications in History), 2000, republished Monash University ePress, 2009.

Davison, Graeme, with Sheryl Yelland, *Car Wars: How the Car Won our Hearts and Conquered our Cities* (Crows Nest, Allen & Unwin), 2004

Elton, Geoffrey R., *The Practice of History* (London, Methuen), 1967.

Foucault, Michel, *Discipline and Punish: The Birth of the Prison* (London, Methuen), 1975.

Guha, Ranajit, ed., *Subaltern Studies* vols I–V (New Delhi, Oxford University Press), 1983–87.

Hobsbawm, Eric, *On History* (London, Weidenfeld & Nicolson), 1997.

Hofstadter, Richard, 'History and the social sciences', in F. Stern, ed., *Varieties of History*, 2nd edn (London, Macmillan), 1968, pp. 359–68.

Isaac, Rhys, *The Transformation of Virginia, 1740–1790* (Chapel Hill, University of North Carolina Press), 1982.

Kitson Clark, George S.R., *The Critical Historian: A Guide for Research Students Working in Historical Subjects* (New York, Garland), 1985.

Ladurie, Emmanuel Le Roy, *The Peasants of Languedoc*, trans. John Day (Chicago, University of Illinois Press), 1974.

Marwick, Arthur, *The Nature of History* (New York, Knopf), 1971.

Mommsen, Theodor, *The History of Rome*, trans. W.P. Dickson (London, Macmillan), 1901.

Munslow, Alan, *Deconstructing History* (New York, Routledge), 1997.

Scott, Joan W., 'Gender: a useful category of historical analysis', in idem, *Gender and the Politics of History* (New York, Columbia UP), 1988, pp. 28–50.

Tosh, John, *The Pursuit of History*, 3rd edn (London, Longman), 1999.

Tosh, John, ed., *Historians on History* (London, Longman), 2000.

White, Hayden, *The Content of the Form: Narrative Discourse and Historical Representation* (Baltimore, MA, Johns Hopkins UP), 1987.

Zeldin, Theodore, 'Personal history and the history of the emotions', *Journal of Social History* vol. 15 (1981–82), pp. 339–43.

Notes

Chapter 1 A History Essay is History

1 Charles Dickens, *Hard Times*, Chapter 1 (opening words).
2 Penelope Lively, 'The presence of the past', *Oxford Today* 16(1) (2003), pp. 26–8 at p. 26.
3 Rees Davies, cited by Vita Hope, 'The past in the present', *Oxford Today* 14(1) (2001), pp. 18–21 at p. 21.
4 On the use of 'he', 'she' and so on as indefinite pronouns, see Chapter 13, pp. 139–40. This book being a guidance manual, the reference of indefinite pronouns in it is generally not to actual individuals but to members of classes (students, teachers, historians etc.); clearly, these may indifferently be male or female, and the pronouns have common gender.
5 The term 'humanities' is sometimes used to identify a grouping of disciplines within a university's organization. It is used here, in its old sense, to identify the study of the products of human culture, and roughly corresponds to the arts, or the liberal arts.
6 This verse, which has several variants, is sometimes attributed to Mrs Craster in 1871, for example by the 3rd edn (but not others) of *The Oxford Dictionary of Quotations*. See also George Humphrey, *The Story of Man's Mind* (Boston, Small, Maynard), 1923, p. 109.
7 This sentence raises a question of grammatical usage which we shall meet later in the discussion of correct English. On the choice of relative pronoun in a defining relative clause, see Chapter 13, p. 140.
8 See, for example, Sarah Barber and Corinna Peniston-Bird, eds, *History Beyond the Text: A Student's Guide to Approaching Alternative Sources* (Abingdon, Routledge), 2009.

Chapter 3 The History Essay as a Process

1 Robin W. Winks, *The Historian as Detective: Essays on Evidence* (New York, Harper & Row), 1969.

Chapter 4 Knowing your Sources

1 This sort of study, piecing together historical knowledge from evidence of births, deaths, migrations, geography, family structure and social interaction, has evolved since late in the twentieth century into a distinct field of scholarship, 'historical demography', influenced by the previous work of the Annales School

in France and furthered by the Cambridge Group for the History of Population and Social Structure. See the work of Simon Szreter, such as his *Health and Wealth: Studies in History and Policy* (New York, University of Rochester), 2005.

Chapter 6 Reading Critically

1   Kalavai Venkat, 'A critical review of Romila Thapar's *Early India – From the Origins to AD 1300'*, *Hindu Review,* 1 July 2003, http://hindureview.com/2003/07/21/critical-review-romila-thapar%C2%92s-early-india-origins-ad-1300/, consulted 19 Jan. 2016.
2   Melanie Phillips, 'Intolerance against religion', *Daily Mail*, 15 March 2002, www.melaniephillips.com/articles/archives/2002_03.html, consulted 26 Sept. 2005.

Chapter 8 Explanation, Judgment and Historical Imagination

1   This is illustrated by the contested question concerning Thomas Jefferson's relationship with his slave Sally Hemings. See Gordon Taylor, 'Teaching history students to read: the Jefferson scandal', *The History Teacher* 22(4) (1989), pp. 357–74.
2   Max Weber, *The Protestant Ethic and The Spirit of Capitalism,* trans. Peter Baehr and Gordon C. Wells (New York, Penguin Books), 2002.
3   An interpretation of Indian cultural attitudes as a response to the hot climate was advanced by the journalist Nirad Chaudhuri, *Hinduism: A Religion to Live By* (Oxford, OUP), 1979.
4   On the role of the uniquely individual character in history, see Theodore Zeldin, 'Personal history and the history of the emotions', *Journal of Social History* 15 (1981/82), pp. 339–43.

Chapter 12 Citing the Sources

1   Kate Turabian, *A Manual for Writers of Term Papers, Theses, and Dissertation,* 8th edn (Chicago, University of Chicago Press), 2013, p. 118.

Chapter 15 Beyond the History Essay

1   Abu'l Fazl, *The Akbarnāma of Abu-l-Fazl,* trans. H. Beveridge (Calcutta, Asiatic Society) 1897, pp. 581f.

Chapter 16 From Essay to Thesis

1   For more detailed advice about the nuts and bolts of research, in history particularly as well as the humanities in general, and in essays as well as in postgraduate work, you may benefit considerably from a readable and encyclopedic guide that has been widely used through multiple editions: Jacques Barzun and Henry H. Graff, *The Modern Researcher*, 6th edn (Belmont, Wadsworth), 2004.

Glossary

Academic writing Essentially, research-based writing in which the author seeks to convince the reader of the correctness of his conclusions by citing verifiably the evidence on which those conclusions are based. The conclusions are fully documented by citation of the sources of evidence, so that the author's claims about what the evidence shows can, in principle, be verified by the reader. If the research is to be fully academic, it must examine the best evidence that is available anywhere for the purpose of supporting answers to the questions addressed. Other forms of writing can also be considered academic, such as book reviews or published lectures; these acquire their academic character because they are informed by the insights gained by their authors from research leading to publications of the sort just described.

Annales School A movement constituted by the work of twentieth-century French historians interested in the detailed analysis of society in the past. It is named after the journal (the *Annales*) in which some of their work was published; it is described further in the Appendix.

Author-date citation A method of citation by which, in parentheses at the appropriate point in a text, the source used is identified by specifying the author's surname and the date of the publication. These items are the key to the full *reference* in the bibliography or list of works cited, placed on a later page.

Bias A tendency to lean to one side. Any historian might have an initial bias towards one side of an argument, as a result either of purely personal attitudes and tastes, or attachment to a particular group – an organization, religious affiliation, nation, language group, sex, educational level, social class, or almost anything else. What matters is whether such leanings interfere with the historian's judgments; we say that his conclusions are 'biased' if his initial inclination interferes with his judgment, preventing him from assessing fairly the evidence on both sides.

Bibliography A list of sources consulted in the writing of an essay, book or journal article. In the case of a journal article (or a chapter or article contributed to a compilation) this list may be entitled 'References', or 'Works cited'.

Citation Identification of a source used. The historian should normally identify for the reader the exact place from which facts or ideas have been drawn. A citation may be provided at the point in a writer's text where the facts or ideas are used, for example by the *in-text* method of citation, or in a footnote. A brief *reference* in either form may need to be supplemented by full details in a bibliography or list of works cited.

Criticism (a) Unfavourable comment, pointing out defects in what is commented on; (b) comment which refrains from taking the work commented on at face value and takes nothing for granted. Meaning (b) is more important in application to the study of history, where the sources read should not be taken at face value; the critical reader should analyse and assess, ready to comment, where appropriate, on the plausibility, intentions, context and implications of whatever the writer says.

Demographic history The study of the history of populations or social groups, examining their structure, family relationships, migrations, physical environments, interactions with government services, employment patterns and so on, particularly as prosecuted by historians influenced by the Cambridge Group for the History of Population and Social Structure, founded in 1964.

Dissertation see Thesis

Document Noun: (a) something written, usually on paper, containing information relevant to a specific purpose; (b) something written, usually on paper, containing historical *primary source* material. A collection of historical documents is a published collection of primary sources for the study of some subject.
Verb: to refer to primary sources, providing citations of sources for them.

Endnote A note containing a citation of a source, placed in a list of references, or bibliography, at the end of an essay, article or book.

Essay A piece of writing expressing what the writer thinks about some subject. Student compositions written as assignments are commonly supposed to be of this form, not simply collecting information but embodying independent critical thought about a topic and generally seeking to construct an argument leading to the answer to a specific question. The element of independent thought is essential to the concept of an essay; therefore 'essay' is used in this book to designate any student assignments having this form, in preference to other designations which may be familiar, such as 'term paper', in order to emphasize that such assignments are exercises in independent thought.

Footnote (a) A note containing a citation of a source used at a particular point in an essay; it may be placed on the same page as the use of the source, or on a later page, in which case it may also be called an endnote; (b) a note of this sort placed at the foot of the page, thus contrasted with an endnote.

Historiography The writing of history. As a topic of study: examination of examples of history writing, from which lessons may be learned about the methods of historical scholarship and the evolution or history of historical scholarship. Often twinned with 'methodology', since the study of works of historical scholarship often overlaps the study of the methods of historical scholarship.

History As a branch of study, it is the study of the past through the critical appraisal of recorded words.

In-text citations A method of citation by which, in parentheses at the appropriate point in a text, the source used is identified by specifying (at least) the author's surname. Different systems may also specify the date of the publication, the page number(s), or both. These items are the key to the full *reference* in the bibliography or list of works cited, placed on a later page.

Literature (a) Verse or prose, particularly writing which deserves to be judged by its qualities of style, clarity, richness, accuracy and so on. A history essay is literature, and should deserve to be so judged. (b) The body of writing of a particular sort, particularly scholarly writing; hence the literature on the civil war is the body of scholarship on the civil war.

Literature review A piece of writing, such as an article, seminar paper, or chapter in a book or thesis, which discusses *critically* the range of historical sources available on a particular topic.

Postmodernism A movement prominent in the work of writers interested in cultural and literary criticism during the last two or three decades of the twentieth century, and to some extent since. It practised critical analysis of concepts in humanities disciplines, generally attacking conventional certainties about objective realities. It has influenced many historians; see the Appendix.

Primary sources Whatever sources count as the raw material for research on a particular topic. Ideally, these are eyewitness reports of whatever events the historian wishes to study; in practice, they are whatever writings are most likely to yield (intentionally or not) good information about the topic in view. They should be broadly contemporary with what is studied.

Public history Recently recognized as a branch of historical scholarly activity with its own needs and character, this is the sort of historical work that goes on outside universities, notably as conducted by people involved in the preservation of cultural heritage, oral history, museology and the protection of historical environments. It often focuses closely on sources for local history.

Reference Identification of a source of information or ideas, usually by citing it in a note; alternatively, the note itself in which a source is cited.

Report A piece of writing in which there is a collection of information, often containing judgments on what the information shows. The focus of a report is the *factual information*; for practical purposes this can be contrasted with an essay, in which the focus is the *independent thought*, the writer's own ideas.

Secondary sources Sources for scholarly writing which are not *primary sources*, but which are written with primary sources as their own sources. Works of scholarship, based on research that uses primary sources, are themselves secondary.

Sources Pieces of writing used as sources of evidence, facts or ideas for the composition of an essay, article or book.

Subaltern studies Studies of culture or society influenced by the desire to shed light on disadvantaged or subordinate classes of the population that are often ignored and written out of history. Such studies were pioneered towards the end of the twentieth century, especially in the study of Indian history; see the Appendix.

Tertiary sources Sources for scholarly writing which are not themselves chiefly or essentially secondary sources. Typically, much of a tertiary source is written on the basis of a critical study of secondary sources rather than on the basis of research using primary sources, with the purpose of producing an account of a broader topic than the author can cover using only the results of his own research. A textbook is commonly tertiary.

Thesis (a) A proposition or conclusion argued for by a teacher or writer, as the main intention of a written work or works; (b) in university procedures (where it may also be referred to as a *dissertation*), a work of this character, generally of book length, based on scholarly research and composed in full or partial fulfilment of the requirements for the award of a postgraduate degree.

Verifiability The possibility of checking that the *sources cited* in a piece of *academic writing* actually support the writer's claims based on them. Checking must be made possible by exact citation of the sources, with all necessary details including relevant page numbers.

Index